THE FATHER'S SPIRIT
OF SONSHIP

THE FATHER'S SPIRIT OF SONSHIP

Reconceiving the Trinity

Thomas G. Weinandy, O.F.M. Cap.

WIPF & STOCK · Eugene, Oregon

Wipf and Stock Publishers
199 W 8th Ave, Suite 3
Eugene, OR 97401

The Father's Spirit of Sonship
Reconceiving the Trinity
By Weinandy, Thomas, O.F.M., Cap.
Copyright©1995 by Weinandy, Thomas, O.F.M., Cap.
ISBN 13: 978-1-61097-083-9
Publication date 11/16/2010
Previously published by T & T Clark, 1995

To St. Athanasius

CONTENTS

PREFACE

This book has one simple objective. I want to argue that within the Trinity the Father begets the Son in or by the Holy Spirit, who proceeds then from the Father as the one in whom the Son is begotten. While a few others have proposed such a view, I know of no book that has taken up this thesis in such a sustained manner. All that I say here seeks to demonstrate the validity and significance of this thesis. My exegesis of the New Testament, my references to the Fathers and other classical authors, and my use of contemporary theologians, are all employed only in reference to this objective. This, then, is not a history of the doctrine of the Trinity, nor a general survey of contemporary trinitarian opinion, although elements of these will be present. This is a work of recommendation. I offer here what I consider to be a reconception of the Trinity.

The stimulus for this work was not expressly trinitarian in origin. I came to this thesis while considering the work of grace in my own life and in the lives of others. As a result of being baptized in the Spirit within the Charismatic Renewal and, after witnessing the changed lives of many others who similarly had experienced this baptism, I was prayerfully considering and studying Romans 8:14–16 – a passage that now possessed experiential relevance: 'For all who are led by the Spirit of God are sons of God. For you did not receive the spirit of slavery to fall back into fear, but you have received the spirit of sonship. When we cry, "Abba! Father!" it is the Spirit himself bearing witness with our spirit that we are children of God.' At one point the thought came to me that if we, who are Christians, are conformed into sons of the Father by the Spirit through whom we are empowered to cry out in the same words as Jesus, then the eternal Son himself must have been begotten and conformed to be Son in the same Spirit in whom he too eternally cries out 'Abba!'

As a consequence of this insight I began to ponder the scriptures and to study the history of the development of the doctrine of the Trinity in its light. I investigated theologians, past and present, to ascertain if I could confirm and corroborate my intuition. I likewise began to consider in depth the meaning, significance, implications, and relevance of my thesis. This work is, then, the fruit of approximately ten years of prayer, thought, and study (although I was baptized in the Spirit in May of 1975). During this time I became convinced that such a thesis had doctrinal, spiritual, and ecumenical importance.

While this book is the result of some earnest thought and arduous work, it was also a joy to write. But then, should not the contemplation of the mysteries of our faith be a delight, especially if the contemplation is that of the immeasurable and unsurpassable font of all the mysteries – the most holy Trinity?

I want to thank the priests of the Mother of God Community in Gaithersburg, Maryland for their encouragement, especially Fr Peter Hocken. I can always count on him to goad me to go a little deeper and become a little clearer than I would have if left on my own. I also want to express my gratitude to Fr Edward Yarnold, S.J., of Campion Hall, Oxford for his critique and counsel concerning earlier drafts. He, and many other members of the Faculty of Theology, have been most kind and gracious to me as colleagues here at Oxford University. I am also very grateful to Dr Gerard O'Reilly of the Oxford English Dictionary for his invaluable service in correcting my grammar and simplifying my style. I also wish to mention Mr Stratford Caldecott of T&T Clark. His confidence in this endeavor has been heartening. Lastly, I want to thank my Capuchin brothers here at Greyfriars, Oxford, and those of my Province in the United States for their fraternal support and care.

I want to end this Preface on an ecumenical note. During the course of writing this book I became ever more burdened by the division between the Roman Church and the Orthodox Churches. I pray that my study will, in some small way, contribute to the mending of the breach. But I am convinced, now more than ever, of the validity of the principle first set forth at the Council of Florence (1438–45) in the midst of laborious and often embittered debate; that is, that the saints of both the East and the West knew and professed the same true faith in the Trinity, and in them we can find our unity of faith. If the wound that continues to impair the unity between the Orthodox and the Latin Churches is to be healed, it will be, not by clever theologians and astute politicians, but by holy men and women who are willing to forgive the past, surmount the present, and contemplate the future glory of the one Church of Christ. I pray that the Holy Spirit, in whom the Father begets the Son, will find our Churches worthy, in our day, of such saints.

Feast of St. Josaphat, 1993

INTRODUCTION

Recently the Trinity has become the focus of renewed theological interest.[1] Specific long-standing concerns as well as fresh theological trends, pastoral circumstances, and movements of Christian renewal have brought this about.

---

[1] For books in English see: Leonardo Boff, *The Trinity and Society* (New York: Orbis Books, 1988); Joseph Bracken, *What Are They Saying About the Trinity?* (New York: Paulist Press, 1979); Joseph Bracken, *The Triune Symbol: Persons, Process and Community* (Lanham, MD: University Press of America, 1985); The British Council of Churches Study Commission, *The Forgotten Trinity* (London: Inter-Church House, 1989); David Brown, *The Divine Trinity* (LaSalle, IL: Open Court, 1985); Bertrand de Margerie, *The Christian Trinity in History* (Petersham, MA: St. Bede's Publications, 1982); Mary Ann Fatula, *The Triune God of Christian Faith* (Collegeville: Liturgical Press, 1990); Bruno Forte, *The Trinity as History* (New York: Alba House, 1989); E.J. Fortman, *Theological Resources: The Triune God* (London: Hutchinson, 1972); Colin Gunton, *Enlightenment and Alienation: An Essay Towards a Trinitarian Theology* (London: Marshall, Morgan and Scott, 1985); Colin Gunton, *The Promise of Trinitarian Theology* (Edinburgh: T&T Clark, 1991); Colin Gunton, *The One, the Three and the Many: God, Creation and the Culture of Modernity* (Cambridge: Cambridge University Press, 1993); Edmund Hill, *The Mystery of the Trinity* (London: Geoffrey Chapman, 1985); William Hill, *The Three-Personed God* (Washington, D.C.: Catholic University of America Press, 1982); Robert Jensen, *The Triune Identity* (Philadelphia: Fortress Press, 1982); E. Jüngel, *The Doctrine of the Trinity: God's Being is in Becoming* (Grand Rapids, MI: Eerdmans, 1976); Walter Kasper, *The God of Jesus Christ* (New York: Crossroad, 1986); Anthony Kelly, *The Trinity of Love* (Wilmington: Michael Glazier, 1989); Catherine Mowry LaCugna, *God For Us: The Trinity and Christian Life* (San Francisco: HarperCollins, 1991); James Mackey, *The Christian Experience of God as Trinity* (London: SCM, 1983); Thomas Marsh, *The Triune God: A Biblical, Historical and Theological Study* (Blackrock, Dublin: Columba Press, 1994); E.L.

Firstly, as a consequence of the renewal of biblical studies with its revitalized understanding of the distinctive roles of the Father, the Son and the Holy Spirit within the New Testament *kerygma*, systematic theologians desire to give trinitarian theology a more biblical foundation. In so doing they hope to breathe new life and relevance into a doctrine that to Christian life and culture has often seemed sterile and inconsequential.[2] The Trinity, as the central mystery of the Christian faith, must not be deemed a mere mathematical riddle (the reconciliation of one and three),[3] but rather

---

Mascall, *The Triune God: An Ecumenical Study* (London: Churchman Publishing, 1986); Jürgen Moltmann, *The Trinity and the Kingdom of God* (New York: Harper and Row, 1981); Jürgen Moltmann, *History and the Triune God* (London: SCM, 1991); John O'Donnell, *The Mystery of the Triune God* (New York: Paulist Press, 1989); Ted Peters, *God as Trinity* (Louisville: John Knox Press, 1993); Karl Rahner, *The Trinity* (New York: Herder and Herder, 1970); R. Swinburne, *The Christian God* (Oxford: Clarendon Press, 1994); John Thurmer, *A Detection of the Trinity* (Exeter: Paternoster Press, 1984); Peter Toon & James Spiceland (eds), *One God in Trinity* (London: Samuel Bagster, 1980); T.F. Torrance, *Trinitarian Perspectives: Toward Doctrinal Agreement* (Edinburgh: T&T Clark, 1994); K. Vasilj, *Trinitarian Theories as Judged by Reason: A New Theory* (Chicago: Ziral, 1987); J.D. Zizioulas, *Being as Communion* (London: Darton, Longman and Todd, 1985).

[2]   Many, if not all, of the works cited in n. 1 stress the need to make trinitarian theology more biblical.

Colin Gunton in his 1992 Bampton Lectures argued that the Trinity must be the basis of human personalism and culture (*The One, the Three and the Many*). See also Boff, *Trinity and Society*.

Pope John Paul II has devoted an encyclical to each of the persons of the Trinity. See *Redemptor Hominis* (1979), *Dives in Misericordia* (1980), and *Dominum et Vivificantem* (1986).

[3]   Kasper states: 'The church's doctrine of the Trinity has obviously never made the completely absurd claim that is constantly attributed to it, namely that 1 = 3. The attribution would be correct only if the doctrine claimed that 1 person equalled 3 persons, or that 1 divine substance equalled 3 divine substances; that is, if it claimed that God is both unity and trinity in one and the same respect. Such a claim would violate the principle of contradiction ... But what the doctrine of the Trinity asserts is that in God there is a unity of substance and a trinity of persons or a unity of substance in a trinity of persons' (*The God of Jesus Christ*, p. 234).

must sustain and nourish the spiritual, but practical, lives of believers. Secondly, the renewal of the liturgy within both the Roman Catholic Church and other Christian denominations has heightened awareness of the importance and presence of the Trinity in personal prayer and communal worship.[4] In accord with the renewal of New Testament studies, the churches and theology recognize today that the early trinitarian faith and proclamation germinated and flourished within a doxological environment (see Mt 28:19; 2 Cor. 13:13).[5] The Church gathers as the people of God in the name of the Father, and of the Son, and of the Holy Spirit, and worships the Father through the Son in the Spirit. The distinctively trinitarian nature of Christian worship has compelled theologians to re-examine the

---

[4] Here I disagree with the BCC report on the Trinity which argues that the recent liturgical renewal in the West has 'made the liturgy less trinitarian' (*The Forgotten Trinity*, p. 6). I would argue that just the opposite has taken place. There has been a renewed focus on the doxological nature of liturgical worship. The Christian community worships the Father in union with the Son by the power and life of the Holy Spirit. Equally the inclusion of the *Epiclesis* within the new Eucharistic Prayers of the Roman Catholic Sacramentary has emphasized that it is the Father, by the power of the Spirit, who transforms the bread and wine into the body and blood of Christ. For a brief statement on the trinitarian nature of the Eucharist see A. Kelly, *The Trinity of Love*, pp. 6–8.

[5] Boff writes: 'So the *liturgy* became the first setting in which faith in the Trinity was expressed. Doxologies (prayers of praise and glory – the meaning of the Greek *doxa*), which we still use in our celebrations, are the earliest testimonies of the recognition of the Trinity in the faith of the believing communities' (*The Trinity and Society*, p. 27).

Sarah Coakley argues that we can find the origins of the patristic doctrine of the Trinity within the early Church's life of prayer and worship, and specifically within this context the development of the personhood of the Holy Spirit. See 'Why Three? Some Further Reflections on the Origins of the Doctrine of the Trinity' in S. Coakley & D. Pailin (eds), *The Making and Remaking of Christian Doctrine: Essays in Honour of Maurice Wiles* (Oxford: Clarendon Press, 1993), pp. 29–56. See also her 'Can God be Experienced as Trinity?', *The Modern Churchman* NS 28 (1986) 11–23.

See also L. Vischer (ed), *Spirit of God. Spirit of Christ: Ecumenical Reflections on the Filioque Controversy* (London: SPCK & Geneva: World Council of Churches, 1981), p. 10.

Trinity in light of these liturgical realities.

Thirdly, the exceptional growth and development of the Charismatic Renewal within all the Christian denominations throughout the world has not only revitalized interest in the Holy Spirit, but also, through the experience of Baptism in the Spirit, fostered a renewed and discernible awareness of the Christian's particular relationships with the individual persons of the Trinity.[6] Baptism in the Spirit has confirmed, in an experiential manner, the love of the Father and the Lordship of Jesus the Son. Thus the Charismatic Renewal has both cultivated and provided factual evidence for the spiritual and practical relevance of the Trinity within the Christian's life.[7]

Fourthly, in light of the above biblical, liturgical and spiritual movements, theologians today emphasize the distinct personalities and roles of the Father, the Son, and the Holy Spirit so as to reverse the impression (often given) that Christians simply worship and relate to the undifferentiated Godhead.[8]

Fifthly, theologians continue to explore the correlation between the economic Trinity and the immanent Trinity.[9] If we are to know

---

[6]   The BCC Study Commission recognizes that the charismatic movement has 'raised urgent questions about the significance of differences of trinitarian belief' (*The Forgotten Trinity*, p. 1).

[7]   I say more about this in Chapter Six.

[8]   Karl Rahner was the first to bring this concern to contemporary consciousness. He stated: 'Despite their orthodox confession of the Trinity, Christians are, in their practical life, almost mere "monotheists"' (*The Trinity*, p. 10).

[9]   Again it was Rahner who first emphasized in contemporary theology the need to model the immanent Trinity upon the economic (see *The Trinity*, pp. 21–38, 101–3. His suggestion has been followed by almost all contemporary trinitarian studies. See, e.g., Boff, *Trinity and Society*, pp. 76, 95, 214–15; Forte, *The Trinity As History*, pp. 7–11; Kasper, *The God of Jesus Christ*, pp. 273–7; Moltmann, *The Trinity and the Kingdom of God*, pp. 158–62; O'Donnell, *The Mystery of the Triune God*, pp. 36–8.

the true God, he must reveal himself as he is in himself. The temporal missions of the Son and the Holy Spirit necessarily disclose the inner life of the Trinity itself.

Sixthly, significant attempts are being made to surmount the ecumenical obstacle of the *filioque* controversy, and thus foster a reunion between the Orthodox and the Catholic Churches.[10]

It must be remembered though that the whole history of the development of the doctrine of the Trinity followed, to a greater or lesser degree, this principle. If it did not, there would be no doctrine of the immanent Trinity. Aquinas, for example, commenting on whether there are processions in God, states: 'As there is an outward procession corresponding to the act tending to external matter, so there must be an inward procession corresponding to the act remaining within the agent' (*Summa Theologica*, I, 27, 1, trans. English Dominican Fathers (New York: Benziger Brothers, 1947)).

LaCugna is one of the few contemporary theologians who wishes to abandon this axiom. The whole of *God For Us* examines instead the relationship between *theologia* and *oikonomia* with regard to the Trinity. I examine LaCugna's position in Excursus Two at the end of the present work.

[10] Besides the works cited in n.1 see, e.g., Louis Bouyer, *Le Consolateur: Esprit Saint et Vie De Grace* (Paris: Les Editions du Cerf, 1980); Yves Congar, *I Believe in the Holy Spirit*, Vol. III (New York: Seabury Press, 1983), pp. 133–214); P. Evdokimov, *L'Esprit Saint dans la Tradition Orthodoxe* (Paris: Les Editions du Cerf, 1969); Jean-Miguel Garrigues, *L'Esprit Qui Dit 'Père!'*: *L'Esprit-Saint dans la Vie Trinitaire et le Problème du Filioque* (Paris: Téqui, 1981); Brian Gaybba, *The Spirit of Love* (London; Geoffrey Chapman, 1987), pp. 119–40; H. Küng & J. Moltmann (eds), *Concilium: Conflicts About the Holy Spirit*, Vol. 128 (New York: Seabury Press, 1979.

See especially the BCC Study Commission, *The Forgotten Trinity*, pp. 30–4, 43; R.P. Jose Saraiva Martins (ed), *Credo In Spiritum Sanctum: Atti Del Congresso Teologico Internazionale Di Pneumatologia*, 2 Vols. (Rome: Libreria Editrice Vaticana, 1982; T.F. Torrance (ed), *Theological Dialogue Between Orthodox and Reformed Churches*, Vols. 1 & 2 (Edinburgh: Scottish Academic Press, 1985 & 1993); Torrance, *Trinitarian Perspectives*; Vischer, *Spirit of God, Spirit of Christ*; K. Ware & C. Davey (eds), *Anglican-Orthodox Dialogue: The Moscow Statement Agreed by the Anglican-Orthodox Joint Doctrinal Commission 1976* (London, 1977).

It should be noted that on significant ecumenical occasions Pope John Paul II has omitted from the Creed the *filioque*, most notably during the celebration of the sixteenth centenary of the Council of Constantinople in 1981.

Recent efforts creatively to address these issues have been inadequate. This inadequacy stems, I believe, from the fact that both the more traditional theologians and even the more progressive ones are working from within trinitarian parameters that are unsuitable to meet the existing biblical, systematic, spiritual, and ecumenical issues. The historical trinitarian development contains within it weaknesses which make true and radical trinitarian enrichment impossible.

The Inadequacies of the Tradition

It is impossible here to trace the history of the doctrine of the Trinity marking both its positive developments and the derivation of its present weaknesses.[11] However, I do want briefly to state and critically to assess the received traditions of both the West and the East, which are founded upon the Nicene-Constantinopolitan Creed and the Athanasian Creed, so as to have a basis for my own study.

Traditionally, Western trinitarian thought, established principally upon Augustine and Aquinas, envisages the Trinity as the Father begetting the Son; and the Holy Spirit, as their communal love, proceeding then from the Father and the Son.[12] As pure relations the Father, the Son, and the Holy Spirit subsist as distinct persons or subjects within the one being of God. These relations establish both their distinct personalities or subjectivities and their oneness

---

[11]   See, for example, the excellent, though at times debatable, study of R.P.C. Hanson, *The Search for the Christian Doctrine of God* (Edinburgh: T&T Clark, 1988). See also E. Hill, *The Mystery of the Trinity*, pp. 45–64; W. Hill, *The Three-Personed God*, pp. 29–80; Kasper, *The God of Jesus Christ*, pp. 249–63; A. Kelly, *The Trinity of Love*, pp. 59–88; J.N.D. Kelly, *Early Christian Doctrines* (London: A. & C. Black, 1968), pp. 83–137, 223–79; LaCugna, *God For Us*, pp. 21–142.

[12]   The commonly accepted view is that Western trinitarian thought begins with the oneness of God and proceeds to consider the distinction of persons, while Eastern trinitarian theology begins with the distinction of the persons and then establishes their unity of substance. I will critically assess this conventional assumption later in this study.

of being. The Father is the Father for he begets the Son and so subsists only in relation to the Son. The Son is the Son because he is begotten and so subsists only in relation to the Father. The Holy Spirit is the Holy Spirit because he proceeds from the Father as his Love for the Son, and in turn proceeds from the Son as his Love for the Father and so subsists only in relation to both. Thus as subsisting relations, both the distinct identities of the three persons and the oneness of their inter-related being are affirmed.[13]

Traditional Orthodox trinitarian thought perceives the Father, as the Godhead, begetting the Son, with the Spirit then proceeding from him through the Son. The East emphasizes that the Father is the sole source of the Son and the Spirit and that the coming forth of the Son and the Spirit constitutes their distinct personalities. The unity of the Trinity is confirmed both in the Father as the fount of the divine processions and in the *perichoresis* of the persons, that is, their intimate inter-relatedness through their mutual inter-penetration or co-inherence.[14]

These two conceptions of the Trinity, forged as they are from scriptural revelation and the conciliar tradition, are the fruit of centuries of theological thought, prayer, and controversy. Now without denying the authentic truth that each proclaims (for to do so would be heretical), I maintain that they are not without defect. To my mind the weakness of both lies in the inadequate, even flawed,

---

[13] For an excellent summary of Augustine's trinitarian thought see E. Hill, *The Mystery of the Trinity*, pp. 75–143, and his introduction to Augustine's *On the Trinity* (Brooklyn: New City Press, 1991), pp. 17–60; and for Aquinas' see W. Hill, *The Three-Personed God*, pp. 62–78.

[14] For an exposition of the doctrine of the Trinity within Orthodox thought see (besides the works listed in n. 10): Vladimir Lossky, *The Mystical Theology of the Eastern Church* (London: James Clarke, 1957), pp. 44–66; John Meyendorff, *Byzantine Theology* (New York: Fordham University Press, 1979), pp. 180–90; and Kallistos Ware, *The Orthodox Way* (London: Mowbrays, 1979), pp. 33–53.

conception of the role or function of the Holy Spirit within the trinitarian life.[15]

Firstly, for the West, the Father and (derivatively) the Son play active roles within the Trinity. In contrast, the Holy Spirit assumes a rather passive function. The Spirit is merely the Love or Gift shared by the Father and the Son. It is therefore difficult to see why, in the Western conception of the Trinity, the Holy Spirit is a distinct person or subject – a who. The Father and Son derive their subjective depth and personhood from their activity. The Father is the Father because he begets the Son and loves the Son he has begotten. The Son is the Son because he loves the Father as an only-begotten. But the Holy Spirit as the Love between them does not play an active role, and thus appears less clearly as an acting subject. He has no subjective depth because he has no defining activity as a person. Why then is the Holy Spirit a person, a subjective 'who', distinct from the Father and the Son?[16]

---

[15] It is commonplace today to say that the Holy Spirit has been in the past the forgotten person of the Trinity. Recently there have been many books on the Holy Spirit to redress the balance. See, for example, Congar, *I Believe in the Holy Spirit*, 3 vols.; F.X. Durrwell, *Holy Spirit of God* (London: Geoffrey Chapman, 1983); Gaybba, *The Spirit of Love*; Alasdair Heron, *The Holy Spirit* (Philadelphia: Westminster Press, 1983); John V. Taylor, *The Go-Between God: The Holy Spirit and the Christian Mission* (London: SCM, 1972); and *We Believe in the Holy Spirit*, A Report by the Doctrine Commission of the General Synod of the Church of England (London: Church House Publishing, 1991). While these and other books creatively address the topic of the Holy Spirit and his role within the economy of salvation, they do so from within the traditional trinitarian framework, with the sole exception of Durrwell who, as we will see, conceives the role of the Holy Spirit in an entirely new light. In light of the contemporary concern for the Holy Spirit, it could now be said that, in most recent theological thought, it is actually the Father who has become the forgotten person of the Trinity. See Thomas Smail, *The Forgotten Father* (London: Hodder and Stoughton, 1980).

[16] For Augustine and Aquinas the Holy Spirit has no proper name, but is designated the Holy Spirit because of what he holds in common with the Father and the Son – holiness and spiritual nature (see *De Trinitate*, V:12; *S.T.*, I, 27, 4, ad 3; I, 28, 4; I, 36, 1). The Holy Spirit is called Love or Gift because he is the mutual

Secondly, while the East has emphasized the distinction of persons, in its legitimate desire to uphold the Father as the sole ungenerate source, it has diminished, like the West, the active roles of the Son and the Holy Spirit within the inner trinitarian life. In addition, the Eastern view of the Trinity is quite linear – the Son is begotten from the Father, and the Spirit proceeds from the Father through the Son. While some positive noetic content can be perceived in the Son's being begotten, the meaning of the Spirit's proceeding from the Father through the Son is indeterminate. What distinguishes 'procession' from 'generation'? What does proceeding 'through the Son' mean? How does this proceeding 'through the Son' effect or determine the personhood of the Holy Spirit? Moreover, this linear view undermines the Orthodox notion of *perichoresis* by which the persons are said to co-inhere in one another. If the movement of the Son and the Holy Spirit is 'out from' the Father, how do they mutually interpenetrate one another?[17]

The reason for these weaknesses, both in the West and the East, resides in the fact that philosophical notions are still active in their respective conceptions of the Trinity which are foreign to and not in accord with scriptural revelation.[18] Specifically, there are traces

---

love or gift shared and given by the Father and the Son (see *De Trinitate*, IV:29, XV:29, 31, 33–6; *S.T.*, I, 37 and 38. Kasper writes: 'The Holy Spirit is pure reception, pure gift ... the Holy Spirit is pure recipient' (*The God of Jesus Christ*, p. 290).

[17] Kasper, in commenting on the trinitarian theologies of East and West, states that, even though the East's understanding is more scriptural and historical than the West's yet, because its conception is linear, 'it formally asserts the inner unity of the three persons rather than makes this unity intelligible from within' (*The God of Jesus Christ*, p. 297).

[18] What makes these philosophical conceptions unacceptable is not their foreignness, but their incompatibility with Christian revelation. Some foreign philosophical concepts may be in accord with revelation, but normally they need to

of Middle and Neo-Platonic emanationism, especially within Eastern trinitarian thought. Similarly, Aristotelian epistemology fashions the Western conception of the Trinity, that is, something cannot be loved until it is known, and thus the Father logically begets the Son before he spirates the Spirit.

Within both views of the Trinity there lingers (reinforced, as we will shortly see, in the West by Aristotelian epistemology) a Neo-Platonic emanationist sequentialism; that is, there is a logical or conceptual priority of the Father over the Son and the Son over the Holy Spirit. (Ontologically, both the West and East would rightly maintain that all three persons are equally eternal.) The Father is logically prior to the Son since he begets the Son, and the Son as first begotten is conceptually prior to the Holy Spirit. Then only does the Spirit proceed: from the Father as his love for the Son and from the Son as his love for the Father, in the West; or from the Father through the Son, in the East.

Particularly in the East's linear view of the Trinity, middle and Neo-Platonic emanationism still governs the trinitarian conception. The Godhead resides in the Father alone, and he shares his divinity with the Son and the Holy Spirit as they emanate out from him in a sequential pattern – first the Son and then the Holy Spirit. This conception, while giving greater integrity to the distinct persons and priority to the unbegotten Father, jeopardizes Nicea's *homoousion* doctrine that the one Godhead resides in and is the inter-relationship among the persons, and not just in the Father alone.

Within Patristic trinitarian theology the use and issue of Platonic emanationism has a long and complex history. The principle of emanation allowed the Apologists and Origen, for example, to give some account of

---

be thoroughly born anew in the water of Christian revelation. Not surprisingly, then, when we come to the Trinity, those philosophical concepts that are drafted into service for use within a trinitarian theology must be radically altered since no secular metaphysics, in its own right, deals with the revelational data of the Trinity. Moreover, the Trinity by its very nature exceeds all human models of understanding.

how the Son and the Holy Spirit could both be distinct from the Father and yet divine in that they shared, through emanation, in his one divine nature. However, this principle could not bear the strain of biblical revelation, which demanded that God be one and that the Son and the Holy Spirit be equally God, for indeed it cannot reconcile, in a conceptually unified manner, the fact that God is one and that the Father, the Son, and the Holy Spirit are God. Emanationism always tended either to tritheism or to subordinationism. Arius, to his credit, perceived that emanationism is incompatible both with revelation and philosophical consistency – the Son cannot emanate from God if God is to be one, for that which emanates out from some source brings division and mutation to the source. Arius resolutely resolved the quandary by thoroughly hellenizing revelation in denying the divinity of the Son and the Holy Spirit and making them both creatures.

The Council of Nicea (325) proclaimed that the Son is truly God. As the Father is God so the Son is God. The Son is *homoousios* (one in being) with the Father. Scholars debate whether or not Nicea conceived *homoousios* as meaning that the Father and Son, as distinct entities, shared the same common divine 'stuff' (which would ultimately be tritheistic) or as designating one and the same reality.[19] For the majority of the Fathers this does not appear to be an explicit question. Their main aim, as witnessed by Eusebius of Caesarea, was to assert the full divinity of the Son.[20] However,

---

[19] See Hanson, *The Search for the Christian Doctrine of God*, pp. 163–72; J.N.D. Kelly, *Early Christian Doctrines*, pp. 231–7; G.L. Prestige, *God in Patristic Thought* (London: SPCK, 1952), pp. 197–218; C.G. Stead, *Divine Substance* (Oxford: Clarendon Press, 1977), pp. 191–266.

Much is made of the fact that seemingly most of the Fathers of Nicea only understood *homoousios* in the generic sense of the Father and the Son sharing the same common divine substance and not in the sense that the Father and the Son are one and the same being. However, since there was the fear, and later the accusation, that the *homoousios* was Sabellian, more of the Fathers must have understood the *homoousios* in the latter sense of 'one being' than is customarily supposed. Only if one conceives the *homoousios* as meaning that the Father and the Son are one and the same being, and not just generically composed of the same common divine 'stuff', could there be any fear or accusation of Sabellianism.

[20] See Eusebius' *Letter to the Church of Caesarea*.

it was Athanasius, who, in his vigorous defense of the *homoousios* against the use of *homoiousios*, grasped that the *homoousion* doctrine demanded that the Father and the Son be one and the same God. The being of the one God is the Father begetting the Son. Thus Athanasius recognized that Nicea's *homoousios* shattered, at least implicitly, but nonetheless absolutely, the Platonic principle of emanation. No longer did the whole of the Godhead reside in the Father alone from whom the Son and the Spirit emanated. Rather the Godhead is the Father begetting the Son. For Athanasius the Son is 'inseparable from the essence of the Father, and he and the Father are one . . . the Word is ever in the Father and the Father in the Word'.[21] *Homoousios* confirms both the full divinity of the Son, and the unity of God, since 'the Son, being an offspring from the substance, is one by substance, himself and the Father that begot him.'[22] 'The Son is begotten not from without [by way of emanation] but from the Father.'[23] The Son 'is proper to and identical with the substance of God and an offspring from it by nature . . . (and) by this fact *homoousios* with him that begot it.'[24] While the Father is the Father and the Son is the Son, they are 'one in propriety and peculiarity of nature, and in the identity of the one Godhead.'[25]

Athanasius' decisive and momentous insight should have transformed the whole history of trinitarian theology. Unfortunately it has not. The Homoiousians opposed Nicea's *homoousios* because they still conceived the Godhead as residing in the Father alone. Thus, to say that the Son was *homoousios* implied for them Sabellianism since this would now mean that the Father and Son were not one and the same substance, but one and the same person. (They were aided in this interpretation by some 'Sabellianizing' supporters of Nicea such as Eustathius of Antioch and Marcellus of Ancyra.) This is why the Cappadocians, especially Basil the Great, sympathized with

---

[21]   *De Decr.*, 20.

[22]   *De Syn.*, 48; see also 53.

[23]   *C. Ar.*, 2:33.

[24]   *Ad Afros.*, 8.

[25]   *C. Ar.*, 3:4.

the Homoiousians. The Cappadocians never captured the true metaphysical significance of Nicea's *homoousion* doctrine. For them the Father alone still embodied the Godhead and the Son was *begotten out of* him and the Holy Spirit *proceeded out of* him. While the Cappadocians were great terminological and conceptual innovators in regard to the Trinity and wished to ensure the monarchy of the Father and true individuality of the Son and the Holy Spirit, yet because they did not possess the metaphysical acumen of Athanasius, Platonic emanationism became firmly grafted into Orthodox trinitarian thought, and it is present to this day.[26]

---

[26] For a more complete study of Nicea and Athanasius' interpretation of it, see Thomas Weinandy, *Does God Change?: The Word's Becoming in the Incarnation* (Petersham, MA: St. Bede's Publications, 1985), pp. 10–16.

David Coffey states: 'As the homoousion in the Athanasian sense coincides materially in designation with the unity of the divine essence, it is evident that the homoousion would have been a more productive basis for continued trinitarian thought than was the actual Eastern starting-point of the distinction of persons; but in the East on the question of the procession of the Holy Spirit the distinction of persons remained the regulative concept despite the development of the homoousion' *(Grace: The Gift of the Holy Spirit* (Sydney: Catholic Institute of Sydney, 1979), p. 8).

On a number of occasions T.F. Torrance sees Athanasius' interpretation of the Creed of Nicea in a manner similar to my own. For Athanasius 'The Logos is *internal* to the Being of God, for God was never without what is properly his own: he is *enousios Logos,* and as such belongs in his own Being to the divine side of the demarcation between the Creator and the creation' *(Theology in Reconciliation* (London: Geoffrey Chapman, 1975), p. 226). Thus Athanasius' interpretation of Nicea's *homoousios* 'meant not merely that the *ousia* of the Son was *of* the *ousia* of God, but that there was an indivisible and continous relation of being of the Father in the Son, so that the being of the Godhead is whole or complete not in the Father alone but in the Son and the Holy Spirit as much as in the Godhead' (ibid., p. 246). Torrance concludes: 'At this point, however, the Athanasian doctrine of God has to be distinguished somewhat from that which came to prevail in later Greek thought through the Cappadocian stress upon the idea that the Father alone is the *arche* ... That way of thinking implied that while the Deity of the Son and the Deity of the Spirit are co-eternal and co-equal with the Deity of the Father, for there is only one Godhead, nevertheless the Son and the Spirit have a *derived* Deity, while that of the Father is *underived* Deity' (ibid., p. 252; cf. pp. 220, 222, 227, 253). Torrance provides many citations from the writings of Athanasius similar to the ones I have cited.

Returning now to the West, this logical, sequential priority of the Father and the Son within Latin trinitarian thought is reinforced by Aristotelian epistemology (which on a human level is correct); that is, by the idea that a thing/person must first be known before it can be loved. Thus the Son is first begotten and known by the Father and then only loved by him in the Spirit who in turn loves the Father by the Spirit.[27] However, I believe that, as the Trinity shatters Platonic emanationism, so too does it transcend Aristotelian epistemology.

Without wishing to deny the biblical imperative that the Son and the Holy Spirit depend upon the Father (otherwise the Father would not be Father), which both the West and East desire to uphold, nonetheless I regard this sequentialism molded by Platonism and reinforced by Aristotelian epistemology as detrimental to a true understanding of the Trinity. A proper understanding of the Trinity can only be obtained if all three persons, logically and ontologically, spring forth in one simultaneous, nonsequential, eternal act in which

See also Torrance's excellent study on how the Fathers themselves interpreted the Nicene Creed: *The Trinitarian Faith* (Edinburgh: T&T Clark, 1988), especially pp. 110–45; and also 'The Triunity of God in the Nicene Theology of the Fourth Century' in *Theological Dialogue Between Orthodox and Reformed Churches*, Vol. 2, pp. 11–12.

See also P. Widdicombe, *The Fatherhood of God from Origen to Athanasius* (Oxford: Clarendon Press, 1994).

[27] Aquinas writes: 'Though will and intellect are not diverse in God, nevertheless the nature of will and intellect requires the processions belonging to each of them to exist in a certain order. For the procession of love occurs in due order as regards the procession of the Word; since nothing can be loved by the will unless it is conceived in the intellect' (*S.T.*, I, 27, 3, ad 3; see also I, 27, 4).

each person of the Trinity subsistently defines, and equally is subsistently defined by, the other persons.[28]

---

[28] I will argue in Chapter Four that while there is an order of origin and derivation among the persons of the Trinity, there is not an order of priority, precedence and sequence. The Trinity embodies or (better) is one simultaneous and harmonious act by which the persons are who they are and they are who they are only in the one act of being interrelated.

CHAPTER ONE:

THE THESIS: BEGOTTEN IN THE SPIRIT

Briefly, the thesis that I wish to put forth in this study, one that may seem subtle, yet one that I believe radically transforms and revolutionizes the Christian understanding of the Trinity, is that the Father begets the Son in or by the Holy Spirit. The Son is begotten by the Father in the Spirit and thus the Spirit simultaneously proceeds from the Father as the one in whom the Son is begotten. The Son, being begotten in the Spirit, simultaneously loves the Father in the same Spirit by which he himself is begotten (is Loved).

The Spirit (of Love) then, who proceeds from the Father as the one in whom the Father begets the Son, both conforms or defines (persons) the Son to be the Son and simultaneously conforms or defines (persons) the Father to be the Father. The Holy Spirit, in proceeding from the Father as the one in whom the Father begets the Son, conforms the Father to be Father for the Son and conforms the Son to be Son for (of) the Father.

This new conception of the Trinity finds its distinctiveness in the specific and precise role ascribed to the Holy Spirit within the immanent Trinity, a role that has been obscure throughout the history of trinitarian theology. By giving the Holy Spirit his proper trinitarian role we more easily recognize his personal ontological depth as a distinct subject. Moreover, the whole Trinity, with the

17

interrelationship of the persons, is reconceived. A fuller statement of this thesis will have to await the course of this essay.

Support and Objections

The formulation of this thesis, as already mentioned in the Preface, has had a rather lengthy incubation. In the initial years of reading and research I did not find any theologian, past or present, who proposed such an understanding of the Trinity.[1] However, I became more and more convinced that the trinitarian tradition, of both the East and the West, was converging upon something like my thesis. This became especially evident when I studied the recent attempts to overcome the ecumenical impasse brought on by the *filioque* controversy. (We will examine these ecumenical attempts in Chapter Five.)

Later, however, I did discover a number of authors who held a similar position to my own. One author admirably argues for my present thesis – F.X. Durrwell.[2] Likewise, Leonardo Boff proposes

---

[1]   At first sight it might appear that Tertullian comes close to the proposed thesis. He writes: 'Discourse, who became Son of God when by proceeding from him he was begotten. "So," you say, "you postulate that Discourse is a sort of substance, consisting of spirit and wisdom and reason (*spiritu et sophia et ratione constructam*)." Certainly' (*Ad Praxean*, 7; translation from *Tertullian's Treatise Against Praxeas*, edited and translated by E. Evens (London: SPCK, 1948)). Or again: 'But the Word consists of spirit, and (so to speak) spirit is the body of the Word (*Sermo autem spiritu structus est, et ut ita dixerim sermonis corpus est spiritus*)' (ibid., 8). While Tertullian here stated that the Son is '*constructam*,' or '*structus est*' in the spirit, this should most likely be taken in the sense that Tertullian, deriving from his Stoic background, understood the nature of God to be a spiritual substance and thus the Word is constructed or formed out of the generic substance of God/spirit (*sermonis corpus est spiritus*) and not from the 'person' of the Holy Spirit. This interpretation would be in keeping with his overall trinitarian thought where the Holy Spirit is placed third in the hierarchical order. The Spirit proceeds from the Father in third place after the Son. 'Now the Spirit indeed is third from God and the Son; just as the fruit of the tree is third from the root, or as the stream out of the river is third from the fountain, or as the apex of the ray is third from the sun' (ibid.).

[2]   See *The Holy Spirit of God*, pp. 133–59.

that the Father begets the Son in the Spirit, though he develops his theory along somewhat different lines from my own.[3] Jürgen Moltmann also proposes the basic thesis in a number of his works.[4] Olivier Clément also briefly speaks of the Son being begotten by the breath of the Spirit.[5] The Church of England Doctrinal Commission also proposes, in harmony with the Orthodox theologian Paul Evdokimov, that the Son comes forth from the Father and the Spirit.[6] Toward the end of my study, I also had the good fortune of speaking with Fr Edward Yarnold, S.J., of Campion Hall, Oxford. I shared with him my proposal. He happily assured me that he had himself proposed the same thesis a number of years ago.[7] While these studies have been of help to me and have reinforced my own thinking, they do not seem to have had any impact on the larger theological community. The significance of what they are proposing appears to have been neglected.

However, the tradition, on the whole, does seem strongly to

---

[3] Boff argues that a true trinitarian theology must embody not only the *filioque*, but also a *spirituque* and even a *patreque*. He does clearly state that the Father begets the Son in the Spirit, and thus *spirituque*. What is not entirely clear is the meaning of *patreque*. Nonetheless, his desire is to uphold the fact that all three persons of the Trinity, within their relationships, in some way help constitute one another. 'In this way we shall have a trinitarian equilibrium since all is triadic and perichoretically implied; all is shared, circulated, reciprocally received, united through communion' (*Trinity and Society*, p. 6; see also pp. 84, 146–7, 204–5, 236). I discuss Boff more fully later on.

[4] See Moltmann, *The Trinity and the Kingdom of God*, pp. 169–70, 182–5; also *The Spirit of Life: A Universal Affirmation* (London: SCM, 1992), pp. 306–9.

[5] See O. Clément, *The Roots of Christian Mysticism* (London: New City, 1993), pp. 58–9, 70, 72.

[6] See *We Believe in the Holy Spirit*, A Report, p. 67.

[7] In 'The Trinitarian Implications of Luke and Acts', *The Heythrop Journal* VII (1966) 18–32.

militate against the proposed thesis. W. Hill, in speaking about the distinction between the Son and the Spirit, states that 'if the Spirit were not from the Son there would be no way of accounting for their distinction (unless the Son were said to be from the Spirit, which has no basis in tradition)'.[8] Gaybba notes that Gregory of Nyssa states, in his *Third Sermon on the Lord's Prayer*, XXXIII, that we can speak of the Son's Spirit but not of the Spirit's Son.[9]

Gaybba also points out that Augustine reminds us that if the Holy Spirit alone were love and not the entire Trinity, then 'the Son would have to be the Son of the Spirit too!'[10] Augustine's own words are:

> If the Holy Spirit alone in that triad is charity, it will immediately follow that the Son is found to be the Son, not of the Father alone but of the Holy Spirit as well. It is said of him in countless places that he is the only-begotten Son of the Father, but without prejudice to the truth of what the apostle says about God the Father: 'Who snatched us from the power of darkness and transported us into the kingdom of the Son of his charity' (Col. 1:13). He did not say 'of his Son,' though it would have been absolutely true if he had said it, because it was absolutely true on the many occasions when he did say it; but he said 'Son of his charity.' So he is also the Son of the Holy Spirit, if the Holy Spirit alone in that triad is the charity of God. If on the other hand this is an absurd conclusion, it can only mean that it is not the Holy Spirit alone who is charity there, but that

---

[8]   *The Three-Personed God*, p. 266, n. 27.

[9]   See *The Spirit of Love*, p. 57.

[10]   Ibid., p. 63.

for reasons I have sufficiently discussed he is distinctively so called.[11]

Gaybba himself states that the Spirit 'is in no way the cause of the Son's existence.'[12] Furthermore, Aquinas' statement, while it concerns the Son being primarily from the Father (which I obviously do not want to deny), seems to undermine my thesis. 'Therefore we must conclude that it is necessary to say that either the Son is from the Holy Ghost; which no one says; or that the Holy Ghost is from the Son, as we confess.'[13] Even more striking is his statement: 'The Apostle calls Christ the Son of the love of God, inasmuch as he is superabundantly loved by God; not, however, as if love were the principle of the Son's generation.'[14]

Finally, LaCugna, in arguing that one cannot thoroughly identify the economic and immanent Trinity, states: 'If every aspect of salvation history were predicated of intradivine life, some absurd conclusions would follow. For example, because Jesus was conceived by the Holy Spirit, it would be necessary to say that the Son proceeds from the Father and the Holy Spirit (*a Patre Spirituque*).'[15]

With the proper nuances, I believe that, despite the evidence of the tradition, my thesis can be sustained. The primary concern of the passages just quoted is to uphold the monarchy of the Father and thus the idea that the Son primarily is begotten from him. This

---

[11] *The Trinity* XV:37, trans. E. Hill, pp. 424–5.

[12] *The Spirit of Love*, p. 153.

[13] *S.T.*, I, 36, 2.

[14] Ibid., I, 41, 2, ad 2.

[15] LaCugna, *God For Us*, p. 220. LaCugna's example – the Incarnation – is one that I will use to show that the Father does beget the Son in the Spirit.

I too wish to support. However, I do wish to say as well that it is by the Holy Spirit that the Father begets the Son.

Presuppositions and Design of the Argument

The following arguments for my thesis are founded upon three interconnected presuppositions. Firstly, the three persons of the Trinity as they reveal themselves in the economy of salvation manifest their inner trinitarian life and relationships. The immanent Trinity is identical to the economic Trinity.[16] Secondly, while the economic Trinity, as revealed within salvation history specifically through Jesus and proclaimed in the scriptures, is expressed primarily in functional and not ontological categories; that is, *ad extra* words and deeds of the Trinity are articulated in relational terms and idioms; yet inherent within these functional categories lies a trinitarian ontology. Functional economic trinitarianism discloses an ontological immanent trinitarianism. The *pro nobis* manifestation of the Father, the Son and the Holy Spirit innately contains and naturally unveils an *in se* ontological reality. Thirdly, the development of authentic trinitarian doctrine and theology is the coming to perceive and express this inherent trinitarian ontology from within its scriptural, and so functional, economic expression.

The design of my argument is threefold. I will examine the New Testament evidence for the thesis of this book using the above

---

[16] Forte writes: 'God in himself and the God who reveals himself are one and the same: the Father through the Son in the Holy Spirit. This correspondence is based on the very mystery of divine fidelity. The Trinity of history manifests itself as the Trinity of glory because "God is faithful and cannot deny himself" (2 Tim. 2:13), cannot deceive us in revealing himself to us' (*The Trinity as History*, p. 8).

Forte also quotes Barth: 'The reality of God in his revelation cannot be isolated – almost as if there were another divine reality beyond his revelation of himself; rather, the exact same reality which we encounter in revelation is his reality in all its eternal depth.' (ibid).

See also those references listed in the Introduction under n. 9.

presuppositions. On the basis of this New Testament evidence, I will then attempt to reconceive, ontologically, the immanent Trinity. Lastly, I will enumerate the implications of this new conception for ecumenism and Christian life.

CHAPTER TWO:

THE NEW TESTAMENT
AND THE TRINITY:
THE EARLY PROCLAMATION

In examining the New Testament evidence for the claim that the Father begets the Son in the Spirit, I will, for the most part, first examine the early Christian *kerygma* concerning Jesus' baptism, death and resurrection as well as the effects of his redemptive work in the lives of believers. Then in the next chapter I will study the Infancy Narratives and the Johannine works since these are considered by most contemporary scripture scholars to be of later development.[1]

The Baptism of Jesus
While the baptism of Jesus provides a prophetic prefigurement of Jesus' whole ministry culminating in his death and resurrection, I am only interested here in discerning the trinitarian pattern.[2] The

---

[1]   My purpose here is not to give a complete scriptural foundation for trinitarian theology, but merely to establish a trinitarian paradigm that will support the thesis of this study. For the biblical foundation of the Christian doctrine of the Trinity, see, e.g., E. Hill, *The Mystery of the Trinity*, pp. 11–41; W. Hill, *The Three-Personed God*, pp. 3–28; Kasper, *The God of Jesus Christ*, pp. 133–43, 163–77, 200–14, 238–51; A. Kelly, *The Trinity of Love*, pp. 28–58; C. Stead, 'The Origins of the Doctrine of the Trinity', *Theology* 77 (1974) 508–17, 582–9; A.W. Wainwright, *The Trinity in the New Testament* (London: SPCK, 1962).

[2]   For a fuller exegetical account of the baptism see Thomas Weinandy, *In*

Synoptics give various accounts of the details of Jesus' baptism. Matthew and Mark state that Jesus himself, upon coming out of the water, saw the Spirit come upon him like a dove. Luke has the Spirit descend upon Jesus after the baptism while he is in prayer, and the dove appears in bodily visible form for all to see. Matthew and Luke objectify the Father's words as if addressed to those around, while Mark has the Father's words being addressed to Jesus personally: 'This is/You are my beloved Son, with whom/you I am well pleased' (Mt 3:17; Mk 1:11; Lk 3:22).[3]

This trinitarian tableau suggests a number of pertinent points. Firstly, the dove hovering over the water is a symbol of God's creative Spirit. Genesis 1:2–3 speaks of God's breath, wind, or spirit (*ruach*) brooding over the waters as God speaks his creative word.[4] Throughout the Old Testament there is an intimate and inborn association between the Word and the Spirit (breath) that issues forth from the one mouth of God. 'By the word of the Lord the heavens were made and all their host by the breath of his mouth' (Ps. 33:6; see Gen. 2:7; Job 33:4, 34:14–15; Ps. 104:30). Through the covenant, God placed his Spirit upon his people, and therefore his words will not depart from them (see Is. 59:21). The prophets spoke God's word because his Spirit came upon them (see Num. 24:2–3; 2 Sam. 23:2; Ezek. 2:1–2, 3:24, 11:5). In Ezekiel 37 we find the creative Spirit of God joined with his prophetic word. The Spirit of God descends upon Ezekiel and he prophesies over the dry

---

the Likeness of Sinful Flesh: An Essay on the Humanity of Christ (Edinburgh: T&T Clark, 1993), pp. 92–8. For the role of the Spirit in the whole of Jesus' earthly life and public ministry, see John O'Donnell, 'In Him and Over Him: The Holy Spirit in the Life of Jesus', *Gregorianum* 70 (1989) 25–45, and Joseph H.P. Wong, 'The Holy Spirit in the Life of Jesus and of the Christian', *Gregorianum* 73 (1992) 57–95.

[3]   All scriptural quotations are from the Revised Standard Version unless otherwise stated.

[4]   See Heron, *The Holy Spirit*, pp. 3–12.

bones and they come back to life.[5]

Now at Jesus' baptism we find, in an unprecedented manner, this same association.[6] God is about to recreate the world as his Spirit hovers over Jesus in the waters of the Jordan, commissioning him to proclaim the kingdom of God.

A trinitarian pattern is clearly discernible. God's creative and prophetic word is always spoken in the power of the Spirit, and as such, in light of the New Testament revelation, we have a clue to the inner life of the Trinity. The breath/spirit by which God speaks his creative word at the dawn of creation and his prophetic word throughout history is the same breath/Spirit by which he eternally breathes forth his Word/Son. As the Father commissioned Jesus by the power of his Spirit to recreate the world so, in the same Spirit, God eternally empowered him to be his Word.[7]

Secondly, the Father speaks as the Spirit descends upon Jesus, declaring him to be his Son in whom he is well pleased. The Father's words are selected from Isaiah 41:4 and 44:2–3 where the prophet speaks of God's suffering servant upon whom he will bestow his Spirit, and the royal enthronement psalm – 'You are my Son; today I have begotten you' (Ps. 2:7).

The sonship of Jesus is here presented as dependent upon his being the bearer of the Holy Spirit. Mark, having the Father address Jesus personally, confirms this emphasis – 'You', upon whom the Spirit is now descending, 'You are my beloved Son.' Through the

---

[5]   Congar has a short but excellent study on the link between the Word and the Spirit in his *The Word and the Spirit* (London: Geoffrey Chapman, 1986), pp. 15–20.

[6]   For the close association between Jesus and the Spirit see, e.g., J.D.G. Dunn, *Jesus and the Spirit* (London: SCM, 1975); Durrwell, *Holy Spirit of God*, pp. 29–58; Gaybba, *The Spirit of Love*, pp. 18–25; Heron, *The Holy Spirit*, pp. 39–60.

[7]   Curiously the opening verses of the Bible may best pictorially illustrate the present thesis. The Father eternally speaks his Word, begets his Son, in the Spirit. I will examine this at greater length later.

anointing of the Holy Spirit, Jesus will remain his faithful servant even unto death. The cross will reveal that Jesus is the Christ (the anointed one) and so the true Son/Servant of the Father (see Mk 15:39).[8] Therefore, as the Spirit conformed Jesus to be the faithful Son on earth, so the Spirit conforms him as the Son, within the Trinity, so as to be eternally pleasing to the Father. Thus the Father's testimony to Jesus' Sonship, in affiliation with the descent of the Holy Spirit, intimates that he eternally authenticates (begets) the Son in the Spirit. The phrase 'Today I have begotten you' is then but a temporal expression of an eternal act. Luke's emphasis on Jesus praying characterizes the eternal communion between the Father

---

[8]   In the Gospels Jesus is presented as the one who continually speaks, acts and lives in obedience to his Father through the Holy Spirit. He is the man of the Spirit (see Mk 1:12; Mt 4:1, 12:28–32; Lk 4:1, 14, 16–21, 10:21; Jn 3:34, 7:37–9; Acts 2:22, 10:38. Also see Durrwell, *Holy Spirit of God*, pp. 30–2; Gaybba, *The Spirit of Love*, pp. 19–21; W. Kasper, *Jesus the Christ* (New York: Paulist Press, 1976), pp. 251, 256; Hans Urs von Balthasar, *Explorations in Theology III: Creator Spirit* (San Francisco: Ignatius Press, 1993), pp. 118–20; Weinandy, *In the Likeness of Sinful Flesh*, pp. 98–108; Wong, 'The Holy Spirit in the Life of Jesus and of the Christian', pp. 57–95. Jesus' life bears testimony that as he lives by the Spirit here on earth, and thus manifests his true nature as Son, so too does he live as Son by the same Spirit within the Trinity.

O'Donnell comes close to the thesis when he writes:

> The Spirit is in him (Jesus) divinizing his humanity and rendering him completely docile to the will of the Father. As such, the Spirit is always the Spirit of Jesus. But at the same time the Spirit is over him. The Spirit makes known to Jesus the will of the Father. Through the Spirit as a unique person or hypostasis Jesus comes to know the Father's will. The nature of his mission unfolds through the impulses of the Spirit which Jesus must follow in obedience even to the point of his death-cry on the cross. In this sense, the Spirit remains the Spirit of the sending Father. But the convergence between the Spirit of Jesus and the sent Spirit of the Father is precisely the Son's yes of obedience. The Son is nothing of himself. *He is from the Father in the Spirit* [emphasis added], 'In Him and Over Him', p. 43.

and the Son in the Spirit.

Thirdly, in the baptism, the same Spirit which confirms Jesus as the beloved equally affirms the Father as the lover. Again this suggests that within the immanent Trinity the Father in begetting his Son in the Spirit constitutes himself as Father by the same Spirit.[9]

The Cross

Only in Mark's Gospel do we find Jesus actually calling God 'Abba', and he does so on the eve of his crucifixion (see Mk 14:36).[10] Here, at the very moment when God looks to be less than fatherly, Jesus, in calling God 'Abba', acknowledges both that God, despite all appearances, truly is his Father and that, in his obedience to the cross, he is the true Son (see Mk 15:39). This 'Abba', spoken from within the passion, reveals the very depth of the Father's and the Son's subjectivity; that is, that they are who they are only in their complete subjective orientation toward one another. The agony in the garden then supremely illuminates the paternity of the Father and the filiality of the Son.

Now, if 'Abba' can only be spoken in the Spirit (see Gal. 4:6; Rom. 8:15), then it is in the crucifixion that we witness most clearly that eternal bond of love forged in the Spirit between the Father and the Son. Within the crucifixion, at this most severe and radical moment, we behold in time the eternal enactment of the Father being ceaselessly, in the Spirit, the Father of and for the Son, and the

---

[9]   Yarnold also argues that this same trinitarian pattern is observed within Luke's presentation of the Transfiguration. While the Holy Spirit is not mentioned, Yarnold concludes that 'it is probable ... that at the Transfiguration the very clear manifestation of the *shekinah* in Luke implies the presence of power and Spirit also, accompanying the words, "This is my Son, my Chosen (or Beloved)" (9:35)' ('The Trinitarian Implications of Luke and Acts', p. 26).

[10]   For studies of Jesus' consciousness of his Father as 'Abba' see J.D.G. Dunn, *Christology in the Making* (Philadelphia: Westminster Press, 1980); J. Jeremias, *The Prayers of Jesus* (London: SCM, 1967); Edward Schillebeeckx, *Jesus, An Experiment in Christology* (New York: Seabury, 1979).

Son being always, in the Spirit, the Son of and for the Father.[11]

It would be useful here to comment briefly upon comparable passages in the Gospel of John. Jesus prays:

> Father, glorify your Son that the Son may glorify you . . . Father, glorify thou me in your own presence with the glory which I had with you before the world was made . . . Father, I desire that they also, whom you have given me, may be with me where I am, to behold my glory which you have given me in your love for me before the foundation of the world (Jn 17:1, 5, 24).

The cross is the hour of Jesus' glory when he will glorify the Father, in that he will complete the work the Father had given him to do (see Jn 17:4, 19:30), and the Father, in turn, will glorify the Son in that through the cross the glory of Jesus, as Son, will be manifested to the world. It is in the extreme humility of the cross that the Son glorifies the Father and the Father glorifies the Son. Again in the cross the eternal drama of the mutual glorification of the Father and the Son (before the foundation of the world) is acted out in time.

Now, the glory that the Father gave to the Son before the world began was given to him 'in love', and if we can equate the Spirit to this bond of love between the Father and the Son (see 1 Jn 4:13), then it is in the Spirit that the Father glorifies the Son and the Son glorifies the Father.

Implicit within the drama of the cross is the eternal drama of the Father humbly giving all that is his to his Son in begetting or

---

[11] The Letter to the Hebrews states that it is 'through the eternal Spirit' that Christ 'offered himself without blemish to God' (Heb. 9:14). As Jesus on the cross offers his life to the Father through the Spirit, so in heaven he eternally, as Son, is wholly focused on the Father in the Spirit. This being Son to the Father, both on earth and in heaven, is possible only because as Son he is fashioned by the Spirit. It is in the Spirit that the Son is stamped or sealed in his subjectivity as Son and so ever disposed to the Father in love.

Forte clearly shows the trinitarian dimensions of the cross. See *The Trinity as History*, pp. 24–31.

glorifying the Son in the Spirit, and the Son humbly glorifying the Father in the Spirit in whom he is begotten.[12] This is precisely what the Spirit will reveal to the world. The Spirit of truth 'will glorify me, for he will take what is mine and declare it to you. All that the Father has is mine; therefore I said that he [the Spirit] will take what is mine and declare it to you' (Jn 16:14–15).[13]

The Resurrection

The New Testament definitively confirms that the Father raised Jesus from the dead (see Acts 2:23, 32, 36; 3:13–17; 4:10; 5:30–31; 7:52; 10:39–40; 13:27–30; 17:31; 1 Thes. 1:10; 1 Cor. 6:14, 15:15; 2 Cor. 4:14; Gal. 1:1; Rom. 4:24, 10:9; 1 Pet. 1:21).[14] By raising Jesus gloriously from the dead the Father has made him Lord (see Acts 2:36; Phil. 2:9–11). By applying Psalms 2, 16 and 110 to the resurrection the early Church perceived that the Father avowed that he could not allow his holy one to see corruption (Ps. 16:8–11), and so raised Jesus up and sat him at his right hand in glory (Ps. 110:1), thus affirming that 'today' (Ps. 2:7) Jesus is his Son and he is his Father (see Acts 2:34–5, 13:33–4; Heb. 1:5, 5:5).

The resurrection, then, bears witness to the inner trinitarian life in that, as the Father glorifies his holy Son in the resurrection, so he equally glorifies his Son through his eternal incorruptible generation. Moreover, the 'today' of the resurrection not only illustrates that Jesus is the eternally begotten Son, but equally

---

[12] See Forte, *The Trinity as History*, pp. 24–31, especially p. 25: 'The Son's way to "otherness", his "handing himself over" to death is a projection into the economy of human history of that which takes place in the immanence of the mystery of God.'

[13] Kasper holds that 'the high-priestly prayer contains the entire doctrine of the Trinity in basic form and in a nutshell' (*The God of Jesus Christ*, pp. 303–6). We will shortly treat more fully the Johannine notion of the Trinity.

[14] Only in the Gospel of John do we find Jesus professing that he has the power to raise himself (see Jn 10:18).

designates and establishes the Father as Father (see Heb. 1:5, Ps. 2:7, 2 Sam. 7:14).

Now, according to Paul, it is 'the Spirit of him [the Father] who raised Jesus from the dead *(to pneuma tou egeirantos ton Iesoun ek nekrōn)'* (Rom. 8:11).[15] Paul preached the gospel concerning the Son who was descended from David according to the flesh and 'designated Son of God in power according to the Spirit of holiness by his resurrection from the dead, Jesus Christ our Lord *(Touhoristhentos huiou Theou en dunamei kata pneuma hagiōsunēs ex anastaseōs nekrōn, Iesou Christou tou kupiou hemōn)'* (Rom. 1:4).

The resurrection strikingly illustrates the same economic trinitarian pattern as found in Jesus' baptism. While it is the Father who raises Jesus from the dead, he does so by the Spirit, and in that act, the Son, who was in the flesh, is now, through the resurrection of that flesh, once again designated Son of God in power.[16]

Because the resurrection has to do with the climactic glorification and empowering of Jesus in the Holy Spirit, it embodies more fully the inner trinitarian relationships. The resurrection, spanning as it does the temporal and the celestial (earthly dead body to heavenly glorified body), becomes the supreme icon of the eternal trinitarian life. As the Father, in the resurrection, testifies that he could not allow his holy one to see corruption and so establishes Jesus in glory through the Holy Spirit, thus confirming that Jesus is his eternal Son, so within the immanent Trinity the Father begets (eternally establishes and confirms) the Son in divine glory and power by the Holy Spirit.[17] Moreover, as the resurrection by the power of

---

[15] In Romans 6:4 Paul writes that 'Christ was raised from the dead by the glory of God the Father.' Here *doxa* could be a Pauline alternative to *pneuma*. We already saw that in Luke there is a close association between *pneuma*, *doxa*, and *dunamis* together with the Old Testament notion of *shekinah* (see Ex. 24:16).

[16] For a good presentation of the trinitarian implications of the resurrection see Forte, *The Trinity as History*, pp. 17–23, 33–52, 91–143.

[17] Durrwell states that 'if he [Jesus] was conceived as Son of God in the

the Spirit absolutely confirms the sonship of Jesus, so it unconditionally confirms, by the same Spirit, the loving eternal fatherhood of the Father.

Becoming Sons and Daughters in the Spirit

Although Jesus' resurrection is the supreme icon of the immanent trinitarian life since it embraces and specifies the personal relationships between the Father, the Son, and the Holy Spirit, yet Christian conversion and the Christian's subsequent life, I believe, offer an even more exact paradigm. As we will see, the paradigm of Christian conversion illumines and interprets the icon of Jesus' resurrection.

When we come to faith and are baptized, we are taken into the very life of the Trinity and establish definable relationships with each of the divine persons. The Christian life is then lived within these specific relationships with the Father, the Son and the Holy Spirit. It is the manner of these relationships and the cause of them that are of interest here.

The Pauline corpus places before us a Christian life that is integrally trinitarian. We, who are baptized, participate in the same transformation that Christ himself underwent through his death and resurrection. We have died with Christ in order that 'as Christ was raised from the dead by the glory of the Father, we too might walk in newness of life' (Rom. 6:4). Therefore, we must consider ourselves 'dead to sin and alive to God in Christ Jesus' (Rom. 6:11). We are no longer in the flesh, but 'in the Spirit, if the Spirit of God really dwells' in us (Rom. 8:9). We were washed, sanctified, and justified 'in the name of the Lord Jesus Christ and in the Spirit of our God' (1 Cor. 6:11). We possess a new covenant with God written in the Spirit (see 2 Cor. 3:6). Therefore, like the risen Christ, we now live

---

Spirit, if he is raised up as Son of God in the Spirit, we can conclude that, in his eternity, theWord is born of the Father in the Spirit' (*Holy Spirit of God*, p. 154; see also pp. 141–2).

a whole new life directly initiated by, and expressly lived in, the Holy Spirit (see Rom. 7:6). God 'gives his Holy Spirit so that we can live a holy life' (1 Thes. 4:8). 'If we live by the Spirit, let us walk by the Spirit' (Gal. 5:25; see also 5:16). The transparent trinitarian pattern that emerges from these and similar passages is that by the Spirit God makes us a new creation in Christ (see 2 Cor. 5:17; Gal. 6:15; Eph. 2:15).[18]

Moreover, because of the Spirit dwelling within us, we are assumed into the very depths of God's inner being – the mystery of God himself. Through Christ we have 'access in one spirit to the Father' (Eph. 2:18). No one 'comprehends the thoughts of God except the Spirit of God', but we have obtained the Spirit of God so as to know the wisdom of God. Through the Spirit 'we have the mind of Christ' (1 Cor. 2:10–16). The inherent logic here is that Christ, having complete access to the Father, comprehends the mind of God because he possesses fully the Spirit of God. We have the mind of Christ, and thus have access to God's inner thoughts, because we too now possess the Spirit. The Spirit, in conforming us to Christ, gives us entrance into God's wisdom.

Furthermore, no longer are we strangers and foreigners, but 'fellow citizens (sumpolitai) with the saints and members of the household (family – oikeioi) of God . . . with Christ Jesus himself as the cornerstone'. We are being built into a holy temple, 'a dwelling-place for God in the Spirit' (Eph. 2:19–22). We have become the innermost sanctuary (naos) where God himself dwells, and therefore we should glorify God with our bodies (see 1 Cor. 3:16, 6:20; 1 Thes. 4:8). Here again, in Christ and through his Spirit, not only does God dwell in us, but we also are incorporated into the familial life of God himself – the heavenly sanctuary or kingdom of God's all-holy being. Thus the Spirit allows us, in our weakness, to pray in conformity with the will of God (see Rom. 8:26–8). In the Spirit we

---

[18] For Paul to live 'in Christ' and to live 'in the Spirit' are closely aligned. See Congar, I Believe in the Holy Spirit, Vol. I, pp. 37–9.

can pray, sing and make melody to God with all our hearts (see Eph. 5:18).

Unquestionably then, this new life that we live with the Father in Christ is founded exclusively on the work of the Spirit. The justification, focus, and ultimate culmination of this new life is comprised in the truth that through the indwelling of the Holy Spirit, received by faith and baptism, we have become sons and daughters of God. 'For all who are led by the Spirit of God are sons of God. For you did not receive the spirit of slavery to fall back into fear, but you have received the spirit of sonship. When we cry, "Abba! Father!" it is the Spirit himself bearing witness with our spirit that we are children of God' (Rom. 8:14–16). Similarly, in Galatians Paul writes: 'And because you are sons, God has sent the Spirit of his Son into our hearts, crying, "Abba! Father!" So through God you are no longer a slave but a son, and if a son then an heir' (Gal. 4:6–7). Equally the splendor of the Spirit allows us to share in the splendor of the Lord so that 'with unveiled face, beholding the glory of the Lord, [we] are being changed into his likeness from one degree of glory to another; for this comes from the Lord who is the Spirit' (2 Cor. 4:7–18; see also Rom. 8:29).

The Holy Spirit, the Spirit of sonship, transforms us into the glorious image of God that is Christ fashioning us into sons of God. This enables us to share an intimate filial relationship with the Father enabling us then to know God as he is – as 'Abba' – and to address him, in prayer and worship, in the exact same manner as Jesus himself – as 'Abba' (see Mk 14:36).

The judgment I wish to secure from the above is unmistakable, The contention of the whole Pauline corpus is that we are taken into the intimate life of the Trinity, becoming genuine adopted sons and daughters of God. We enjoy the same rights and privileges as Jesus. We experience a heavenly life analogous to his own. It is the Holy Spirit alone who effects and sustains this life with the Father in Christ. But if we are begotten as children of the Father expressly by the Holy Spirit, and if our life with the Father in Christ is sustained solely in the Spirit, then *ipso facto* the Son himself necessarily is begotten by the Father in the Holy Spirit and eternally lives as the divine Son in the Spirit. It is inconceivable, especially if we assume that the persons of the Trinity reveal themselves as they are in themselves and so act in accordance with their singular personalities (to do otherwise would not be revelation at all), thus acting *ad extra* as they act *ad intra,* that we would become sons and daughters of the Father in a manner different from that in which the eternal Son becomes Son.[19]

Furthermore, the Spirit is designated as the 'Spirit of the Son'. Traditionally this has been interpreted by the West as implying that the Spirit proceeds from the Son as well as from the Father since the Spirit is the Son's Spirit. This is a legitimate interpretation. However, since the Spirit of the Son makes us sons, it would seem to imply that 'Spirit of the Son' can equally be interpreted as the Spirit by which the Son is Son – the Spirit of sonship, the Spirit which forms or conforms someone into a S/son.

Moreover, the Holy Spirit in transforming us into children of God and so empowering us to call God 'Abba', highlights our new intimacy with the Father. By being related to the Father in a new way, the Father in turn is related to us in a new way – now as Father. This is presupposed in the above quotes and made explicit by Paul

---

[19]   David Coffey makes a similar inference, but does not actually conclude that the Son therefore must be begotten in the Spirit:

> We have received, ultimately from the Father, a bestowal of the Holy Spirit which makes us sons and daughters of the Father and draws from us a response of love for the Father. The innate unitiveness of the Father's love, which is the Holy Spirit, is actualized fully only in our response, which is a human love enabled, elicited, and sustained by the Holy Spirit active within us. If this is true of the 'sons in the Son,' how much more so of the divine Son himself! As his Sonship is unique, so must his response, the love which he returns to the Father, be unique. ('The "Incarnation" of the Holy Spirit in Christ', *Theological Studies* 45 (1984) 475).

when he states that the love of God is poured into our hearts through the Holy Spirit (see Rom. 5:5). The Spirit then not only allows us to call the Father 'Abba', but it is the same Spirit that reveals the Father as 'Abba', *for us*. Without this 'Abba'-Spirit neither would God be 'Abba', loving us as a Father, nor would we be able to call him in love, 'Abba'. Analogously then, we can conclude that as the Holy Spirit makes God 'Abba' for us *ad extra* so he conforms the Father as 'Abba' to the Son within the immanent Trinity as well. As the Spirit of sonship conforms the Son to be Son (love for the Father is the essence of sonship), so the Spirit of the Father conforms the Father to be Father (love for the Son is the essence of fatherhood).

For Paul, what has begun here on earth finds its completion in our own resurrection. God chose us from the beginning 'to be saved, through sanctification by the Spirit' so that we 'might obtain our glory of the Lord Jesus Christ' (2 Thes. 2:13–14). Through the Spirit God reveals to us what eye has not seen and ear has not heard (see 1 Cor. 2:9–10). In this life we groan in the Spirit awaiting our full adoption as sons even now being 'conformed to the image of his Son, in order that he might be the first-born among many brethren' (Rom. 8:29; see also Rom. 8:23; 2 Cor. 1–5). 'Through the Spirit, by faith, we wait for the hope of righteousness' (Gal. 5:5). If we are transformed into children of God by the Holy Spirit, then we become heirs, 'heirs of God and fellow heirs with Christ' (Rom. 8:17; see also Gal. 4:7). Again it is the Holy Spirit that guarantees our inheritance as the Father's children, the very same Spirit that made Christ himself an heir. If God raised Jesus from the dead by the power of the Holy Spirit, that same Spirit, dwelling in us, will raise us up as well (see Rom. 8:11; Phil. 3:21). The Holy Spirit is the guarantee, the first down payment, the seal of our future inheritance for the day of our redemption (see Rom. 5:5–10; 2 Cor. 1:22; Eph. 1:13, 4:30). 'He who sows to the Spirit will from the Spirit reap eternal life' (Gal. 6:8).

Our own resurrection, then, the fulfillment of our being made sons by the Holy Spirit, reinforces both our present conclusions and our earlier interpretation of Jesus' own resurrection, in that both reflect the eternal begetting of the Son in the Spirit. Our resurrection confirms that we are indeed adopted sons of the Father begotten in the Spirit. Our resurrection in the Spirit then becomes an icon of Jesus' resurrection in the Spirit, but because of this we see more clearly that his own resurrection is then the supreme icon of the inner trinitarian life. If our sonship is established in the Holy Spirit and finds its resurrected completion in the Holy Spirit, mirroring the work of the Spirit in Jesus' own resurrection, we have a transparent window into the work of the Spirit within the Trinity. Reversing the argument, if the Father raises both Jesus and us to glory by the Holy Spirit, and our resurrection is founded on our being adopted as sons by the Holy Spirit, then Jesus' resurrection not only establishes him as Son in power in the Spirit, but equally manifests (in a manner analogous to our own adopted sonship) his being son by nature in the Spirit.[20]

Conclusion

In this chapter we have found that the early strata of New Testament evidence support the thesis that the Father begets the Son in the Spirit. This was exemplified both within the life of Jesus himself and in our own lives as Christians. We must now proceed to the later New Testament development.

---

[20]   I have not taken up the question whether Paul conceived the Spirit as an impersonal power or a personal subject. For a discussion of this see Gaybba, *The Spirit of Love*, pp. 31–4 and Kasper, *The God of Jesus Christ*, pp. 210–14.

CHAPTER THREE:

THE NEW TESTAMENT
AND THE TRINITY:
THE LATER PROCLAMATION

In this chapter I want to examine what most contemporary scholars believe to be later New Testament developments. The Infancy Narratives developed out of prayerful reflection upon the public ministry of Jesus and especially upon his death and resurrection, and thus while first in chronology are later faith formulations.[1] Similarly the Johannine corpus, while founded upon the earlier apostolic proclamation, is believed by most scholars to reflect later theological development. I will conclude this chapter with a short study of some of the trinitarian doxologies contained in the New Testament.

The Infancy Narratives
A detailed exegesis of the Infancy Narratives is beyond the scope of this study.[2] Rather the aim, as in the previous chapter, is to discern,

---

[1]   We should not think, however, that the early Church 'fabricated' the events of his conception and birth in light of the cross and resurrection, but rather used these later events of Jesus' earthly life as the interpretive tool for understanding the true nature of what had happened at the beginning of his life.

[2]   See, e.g., Raymond Brown, *The Birth of the Messiah* (New York: Doubleday,

for the purpose of the present thesis, the trinitarian pattern portrayed in these narratives.

The Gospel according to Matthew tells us: 'Now the birth of Jesus Christ took place in this way. When his mother Mary had been betrothed to Joseph, before they came together she was found to be with child of the Holy Spirit *(ek pneumatos hagiou)*' (Mt 1:18). Similarly, the angel of the Lord appeared to Joseph in a dream and assured him that that which 'is conceived in her is of the Holy Spirit *(ek pneumatos estin hagiou)*' (Mt 1:20). Two points can be made here.

Not only is Jesus said to be 'of the Holy Spirit', but also, and secondly, it was the angel of the Lord *(angelos kuriou)* who made this known to Joseph. In the Old Testament, angels, in order to protect the transcendent otherness of God, originally stood for God himself – Yahweh (see Gen. 16:7, 22:11; Ex. 3:2; Judg. 2:1). Moreover, *kurios* (Lord) was the Septuagint translation of the Hebrew *Yahweh*.

Moreover then, Mary shall ' "conceive and bear a son, and his name shall be called Emmanuel" (which means, God with us)' (Mt 1:23; see Is. 7:14). The identification of the child as 'a son' refers chiefly to his human maleness. However, the conception of this son by the Holy Spirit (authenticated for Matthew in that Joseph and Mary did not have relations prior to his birth, see 1:24–5) confirms that he will be called 'God-with-us', and so intimates that Mary's son is equally, in some sense, a divine Son. The fact that Joseph is to name this child 'Jesus' ('Yahweh saves'), since he will save the people from their sins, lends further support to the divine status of Jesus' sonship. In the Old Testament Yahweh is the only one who can save from sin (see Pss. 51, 130).

We cannot infer too much from Matthew's Infancy Narrative, but at least we can discern a nascent trinitarian pattern. Jesus was conceived of the Holy Spirit, and Yahweh (the Father) was instrumental in his conception to the extent that he sanctioned it in

1977); and René Laurentin, *The Truth of Christmas* (Petersham, MA: St. Bede's Publications, 1986).

his confirmation to Joseph. Therefore the S/son born of Mary manifests God-with-us.

Luke's account of the conception of Jesus illustrates this trinitarian paradigm more clearly. In response to Mary's question as to how she can conceive, since she has no husband, the angel Gabriel (sent by God and so again the representative of Yahweh) assures her that 'The Holy Spirit will come upon you *(pneuma hagion epeleusetai epi se)*, and the power of the Most High will overshadow you; therefore the child to be born will be called holy, the Son of God' (Lk 1:35).

Now the child will be holy *(hagion)*, an attribute accorded exclusively to God in the Old Testament (see 1 Sam. 2:2; Ps. 33:21, 71:22; Hos. 11:9; Is. 5:24, 6:3; Heb. 3:3), precisely because he is conceived by the Holy Spirit, who equally possesses this divine quality.[3]

Moreover, the power of the Most High *(dunamis hupsistou)*, that is, the Holy Spirit of Yahweh (the Father), will overshadow *(episkiasei)* Mary.[4] This is an allusion to Exodus 40:34–5 where the glory of the Lord (the *shekinah*) filled the tabernacle in the form of a cloud.[5]

This descriptive picture discloses why Jesus will be called the Son of God. Firstly, because he is conceived by the Holy Spirit, he possesses the very holiness of God and therefore is God. Secondly, Mary, as the new ark or tabernacle, bears within her the very presence

---

[3]   See Durrwell, *Holy Spirit of God*, pp. 13–15.

There are only three places in the Old Testament where the Spirit of God is referred to as 'the Holy Spirit' (Is. 63:10; Ps. 51:11; Wis. 1:5). Gaybba speculates that the Spirit was called Holy Spirit at the end of the Old Testament era because the people had ceased to pronounce God's name – Yahweh. 'They would therefore no longer talk of *God's* Spirit, but rather of the *holy* Spirit. The world "holy" made it clear that the Spirit spoken about belonged to God' *(The Spirit of Love*, p. 11).

[4]   Yarnold shows that there is a close association in Luke between *dunamis* and *pneuma*. See 'The Trinitarian Implications of Luke and Acts', p. 22.

[5]   Luke uses the same Greek word for *shekinah* as the Septuagint.

and glory of God.[6]

What is significant here is the trinitarian pattern woven within Matthew's and Luke's Infancy Narratives.[7] While these passages are primarily concerned with the human conception of Jesus in the womb of Mary, yet because the son conceived in her is none other than the holy Son of God, the roles played by the Father, the Son, and the Holy Spirit in this decisive moment within the economy of salvation provide testimony for the roles they perform within the Trinity itself.

The depiction of the Father begetting his Son in the womb of Mary by the Holy Spirit becomes, I believe, a temporal icon of his eternally begetting the Son by the Holy Spirit. Firstly, as the Son is sent forth from the Father into the world by the power of the Holy Spirit, so the Son is eternally begotten of the Father in the Holy Spirit. Secondly, as the Son is conceived in the womb of Mary by the power of the Holy Spirit, and so conforms the Son to be Son now as man, so the Holy Spirit conforms the Son to be the eternal Son of the Father within the immanent Trinity.[8] Thirdly, as the economic 'sending' of the Son, effected by the power of the Holy Spirit, a mission for the forgiveness of sins, makes the Father *our* Father, so

---

[6]   Luke's Infancy Narrative asserts Jesus' divine sonship in other respects as well. See Laurentin, *The Truth of Christmas.*

[7]   Yarnold paraphrases Gabriel's response to Mary: 'God's creating spirit will come upon you; the creative power of God will overshadow you, as the cloud overshadowing the tent indicated God's presence. Therefore, though you are a virgin, you will conceive, and your son will have God for his Father, and he will share his father's holiness' ('The Trinitarian Implications of Luke and Acts', p. 23).

[8]   Hans Urs von Balthasar speaks of a 'soteriological' or 'trinitarian' inversion. By this he means that, whereas in the immanent Trinity the Father and Son are the active principles in that they love one another in the Holy Spirit, in the economic Trinity the Holy Spirit becomes an active principle in that it is through the Spirit that the Son becomes incarnate in the womb of Mary and it is by the activity of the Spirit that Jesus obeys the Father and so accomplishes the work of redemption. 'But in this surrendering himself, the Son, the incarnate One, becomes in one respect a product of the Holy Spirit who brings him forth *ex Maria Virgine*, although within

similarly, within the immanent Trinity, the Spirit by which the Father begets his Son is the same Spirit by which he himself becomes the Father *of* the Son.[9]

The Johannine Literature

The Gospel of John affords further evidence of this same trinitarian pattern, specifically as it relates to believers sharing in the very life of God.

The Synoptics tell us that Jesus baptizes with the Holy Spirit precisely because he possesses the fullness of the Spirit (see Mt 3:11; Mk 1:8; Lk 3:16). The Gospel of John elaborates this point more fully and clearly: 'For he whom God has sent utters the words of God, for it is not by measure that he gives the Spirit; the Father loves the Son, and has given all things into his hand' (Jn 3:34–5). John the Baptist professed:

> I saw the Spirit descend as a dove from heaven, and it remained on him. I myself did not know him; but he who sent me to baptize with water said to me, 'He on whom you see the Spirit descend

---

the Trinity itself the Spirit is the product of the united spiration of the Father and the Son' *Theo-Drama*, Vol. III (San Francisco: Ignatius Press, 1992), p. 186. Thus within the immanent Trinity the Spirit is passive-receptive. Within the economic Trinity the Son is passive-receptive. See also *Theo-Drama*, Vol. III, pp. 183–91, 520–3. See also O'Donnell, 'In Him and Over Him: pp. 28–9.

Von Balthasar needs to posit this 'trinitarian inversion' precisely because he does not grasp that the Holy Spirit is active within the immanent Trinity in a manner similar to the manner in which he is active within the economic Trinity. It is because the Father begets the Son in the Spirit that the Father incarnates the Son by the same Holy Spirit.

[9]   Again Coffey comes close to drawing the same conclusion as my own. 'If Jesus is brought into being as the divine Son in humanity through the Father's radical bestowal of love on him, which love is the Holy Spirit, and if the response of Jesus is a love for the Father which ultimately is a return of this same Spirit, then in the immanent Trinity itself the Holy Spirit exists as the mutual love of the Father and the Son' ('The "Incarnation" of the Holy Spirit in Christ', pp. 479–80). Cf. D. Coffey, 'A Proper Mission of the Holy Spirit', *Theological Studies* 47 (1986) 234.

and remain, this is he who baptizes with the Holy Spirit.' And I have seen and have borne witness that this is the Son of God (Jn 1:33–4).

This 'remaining' or abiding of the Spirit with Jesus is the Father's confirmation that Jesus, the one to whom he has given the Spirit without measure, is he who will baptize in the Spirit. Moreover, he will do so only because, as the bearer of the Spirit, he is the eternal Son of God. For John the Baptist, the descent and abiding of the Spirit upon Jesus reveals that he is the baptizer in the Spirit and thus is the Son.

It would seem to follow that as the Father confirms Jesus as the baptizer in the Spirit and so reveals him to be his Son possessing the fullness of the Spirit (it is for this reason that he is the baptizer), so within the Trinity it is the Father who begets his Son in the Spirit. It is because the Father begets Jesus in the Spirit that he possesses the Spirit without measure (the Spirit of Sonship), and thus is able, as the Son incarnate, to baptize with the Spirit, making those so baptized sons.

The Gospel of John contains other similar patterns of trinitarian thought. For example, Jesus assures Nicodemus that 'unless one is born of water and the Spirit, he cannot enter the kingdom of God. That which is born of the flesh is flesh, and that which is born of the Spirit is spirit' (Jn 3:5–6). The Holy Spirit is the very divine life now shared with us so that we might newly participate in the intimate life of God himself.

Likewise, Jesus tells the Samaritan woman that the water he gives 'will become in him a spring of water welling up to eternal life' (Jn 4:14). At the Feast of Tabernacles, a feast celebrating Israel's life with God established in the covenant and secured in God's abiding presence in the temple (see 1 Kgs. 8; 2 Sam. 6; Dt. 31:10ff.), Jesus again proclaims 'If anyone thirst, let him come to me, and let him who believes in me drink. As the scripture has said, "Out of his heart shall flow rivers of living water"' (Jn 7:37–8).[10] John equates the 'living water', which gushes forth from Jesus, with 'the Spirit' whom those who believe in Jesus would receive, 'for as yet the Spirit had not been given, because Jesus was not yet glorified' (Jn 7:39). Again these passages speak of the Spirit as the bounteous source of our abiding and eternal life with God.

Is there a similarity in John between what the Spirit does for us through faith in Jesus and what the Spirit does for Jesus himself? When Nicodemus asked how he can be born anew, Jesus answered: 'Truly, truly, I say to you, we speak of what we know, and bear witness to what we have seen; but you do not receive our testimony. If I have told you earthly things and you do not believe, how can you believe if I tell you heavenly things?' (Jn 3:11–12). What does Jesus know? What has he already seen to which he now bears witness? What testimony do Nicodemus and others not receive? If Nicodemus finds it difficult to believe that he can be born of the Spirit (something that takes place on earth), what heavenly things will he find even more incredible? The answer, I submit, is that Jesus himself knows and has experienced that to which he now bears witness because he is himself eternally born in the Spirit and therefore is the Son of God who comes from the Father; and this is what (in John) the Jewish leaders obstinately refuse to believe and the reason why Jesus is ultimately condemned (see Jn 19:7). As Son, Jesus was never of the flesh. He was always born of the Spirit, and thus eternally resides

---

[10]   Scripture scholars debate whether or not John 7:37–8 should be translated as the 'rivers of living water' flowing from the heart of Jesus or from within those who believe. Today most scholars prefer the former reading (see Congar, *I Believe in the Holy Spirit*, Vol. I, p. 50). This translation would seem to be more in accord with the rest of the Gospel where the Spirit is said to abide within Jesus (Jn 1:33–4); that Jesus is the source of living water (Jn 4:10), and especially that water flowed from the side of Jesus on the cross (Jn 19:34). If, then, the living waters of the Spirit flow from the heart of Jesus, it would seem to imply that it is the Spirit who molds and suffuses the very being, the very heart, of Jesus, and so conforms Jesus to be who he is – the Son. Only because the Spirit wells up in him as the Son can he then baptize with the Holy Spirit.

as Son in the kingdom of God, that is, within the trinitarian life. Our earthly birth in the Spirit mirrors Jesus' heavenly birth in the Spirit.

The First Letter of John underscores this in a more theological manner. Those who believe that Jesus is the Son and keep his command of love will abide in God and God in them. 'We know that he abides in us, by the Spirit which he has given us' (1 Jn 3:24; see also 4:13). Moreover, 'Whoever confesses that Jesus is the Son of God, God abides in him, and he in God. So we know and believe the love God has for us. God is love, and he who abides in love abides in God, and God abides in him' (1 Jn 4:15–16). The Spirit, in these passages, is the bond of love, given to us by God upon faith in the Son, by which God abides with us and we with God (see Jn 14:23). To possess the Spirit is to abide in love and thus to abide in God who is love.

Now, if through faith in the Son, we are united to the Son, and so abide in God as God is, which is the whole point of the proclamation (analogous then to the manner in which the Son himself abides with God), and if we do so through the Spirit of love, then it would appear that the Son himself eternally abides with the Father by this same Spirit of love. Jesus prayed that 'the love with which you [Father] have loved me may be in them, and I in them' (Jn 17:26). The same Spirit by which we become one with the oneness of the Father and the Son, is the same Spirit by which they themselves are one. As our oneness with God, our abiding, is founded upon the Spirit given to us by the Father, so the Son's oneness with the Father is established by the Spirit in which he is begotten and in which he eternally abides with the Father in love.[11]

---

[11] There is a similar line of argument when in John's Gospel Jesus promised his disciples that the Father would send another Counsellor (*parakletos*), 'even the Spirit of truth, whom the world cannot receive, because it neither sees him nor knows him; you know him, for he dwells with you and will be in you' (Jn 14:16–17). The implication is that Jesus does see and know the Spirit. Furthermore, we will know the Spirit for, like Jesus, he will now dwell in us. Thus if our knowledge of the Spirit is founded on the Spirit transforming us through his indwelling, it

A similar line of argument can be found concerning the Spirit as the Spirit of truth. The Spirit of truth, whom Jesus will send and who proceeds *(ekporeuetai)* from the Father will bear witness to Jesus (see Jn 15:26). The Spirit of truth will convince the world of sin for its refusal to believe in Jesus; of righteousness, for Jesus goes to the Father; and of judgment, for Satan is sentenced (see Jn 16:7–11). The Spirit of truth then will confute all that is false concerning Jesus and his identity – lack of faith in him as the Son of God, and Satan, the Father of lies. Moreover, he will positively testify to the Father's judgment of Jesus' righteousness as his true and faithful Son. When the Spirit of truth comes, he will guide the disciples to all truth,

> for he will not speak on his own authority, but whatever he hears he will speak, and he will declare to you the things that are to come. He will glorify me, for he will take what is mine and declare it to you. All that the Father has is mine; therefore I said that he will take what is mine and declare it to you (Jn 16:12–15).

Jesus prays to the Father on behalf of his disciples: 'Sanctify them in the truth; your word is truth. As you send me into the world, so I have sent them into the world. And for their sake I consecrate myself, that they also may be consecrated in the truth' (Jn 17:17–19). Who then overcomes the world? 'He who believes that Jesus is the Son of God.' The Spirit (along with the water and the blood) 'is the witness, because the Spirit is the truth'. Ultimately this is 'the testimony of God that he has borne witness to his Son', and to believe the Father's testimony is to have eternal life, for this life is 'in the Son. He who has the Son has life' (1 Jn 5–12).

From this complex array of texts a distinctive trinitarian pattern emerges.[12] Firstly, the Spirit proceeds from the Father as the Spirit

---

would seem that Jesus' own knowledge of the Spirit resides in the Spirit equally conforming him as Son in the Spirit.

[12] Congar provides a schema of texts in John's Gospel which shows the

of truth and thus, through the Spirit, the Father testifies to the truth that Jesus is the Son. The Spirit himself, as the Spirit of truth, bears witness to Jesus, but he does so from what he has himself heard from the Father. The Father glorifies Jesus, but he glorifies Jesus in and through the testimony of the Spirit ('the Spirit will glorify me'), for all that the Father has given to Jesus as his own, the Spirit will take and declare to the disciples. The glory, which Jesus possessed before the world was made, conferred by the Father and testified to by the Spirit, is that he is the Son. Jesus, through the Spirit, consecrated himself in this truth – through his life and death – and now the same Spirit sanctifies and consecrates believers in this identical truth.

Secondly, and most obviously, the Spirit is designated throughout as the Spirit of truth. The Spirit is the Spirit of truth because he testifies to the truth. God's word is truth. Jesus as the Word of God is the truth of God (the source of all truth) to which God's Spirit of truth bears witness.

Again I would want to argue that implicit within this Johannine economic trinitarian pattern is the implication that the Father eternally glorifies/begets/speaks his Word of truth in or by the Spirit of truth. As the Spirit of truth now bears witness on earth to the truth of Jesus' eternal sonship, so the authenticity and reality of this sonship – its truth – conferred by the Father, is conformed in the Spirit – in truth. Moreover, as the Spirit of truth fashions Jesus into the Word of God, so the Spirit of truth conforms the Father into the Truth-Speaker. The Father is the Truth-Speaker and the Son is the true Word only because the Father speaks his Word, by which he becomes Father, by the breath of the Spirit of truth.[13]

By way of conclusion to this section, the Johannine literature makes two declarative statements about the nature of God. 'God is

---

relationship of the Spirit to the Father and to the Son, the actions attributed to the Spirit, and the parallel activities of the Spirit and the Son (see *I Believe in the Holy Spirit*, Vol. I, pp. 54–5).

[13]   In John a number of concepts seem to cluster around the Holy Spirit –

spirit' (Jn 4:24) and 'God is love' (1 Jn 4:8, 16). Traditionally these passages have been interpreted as statements about the common nature of the one God; that is, God's nature is incorporeal and thus God is a spiritual being, and the essence of God's nature is to love. In light of the above, I believe that such interpretations, while true, nonetheless inhibit our understanding of the deeper and authentic significance of what John is actually declaring.

Jesus told the Samaritan woman that the hour had arrived when 'the true worshipers will worship the Father in spirit and truth, for such the Father seeks to worship him. God is spirit, and those who worship him must worship in spirit and truth' (Jn 4:23–4). The implication is that until now the Father was not truly worshiped in spirit and truth. But if we merely interpret 'God is spirit' to mean God is a spiritual being, then the Jews already did worship God in spirit and truth, because they already knew God to be incorporeal

---

glory, truth, life, light, and love. Their inter-relatedness and their foundation in the Spirit is beyond the scope of this study, yet I believe that such a study might show, as is evident from my brief investigation of 'love' and 'truth', that these come forth from the Father and find their perfect expression in the Son *by the Holy Spirit*. The Father and Son are in one another and thus are one because the Father begets (speaks, glorifies, and gives life to) the Son in love and truth by the Holy Spirit. The prologue of John, for example, declares that the Word who was with God and was God is life and light. This Word became flesh and we have seen therefore the glory of the only Son, full of grace and truth. John the Baptist is a witness to all this precisely because he saw the Spirit descend upon Jesus and abide with him. The Spirit confirms that Jesus is the Son of God possessing all the above attributes (see Jn 1:32–4). Does this confirmation by the Spirit, within the economy of salvation, illustrate the Father bestowing upon the Son these attributes in the Spirit within the immanent Trinity? I believe so. Durrwell argues that all of the attributes of God – power, holiness, glory, life, spirit, love – are *personified in the Spirit*, who is God himself in the depths of his being' (*Holy Spirit of God*, pp. 20–1; see also pp. 8–28, 162).

I would also fully support Kelly's claim that 'any distinction between ontological and functional Christology or trinitarianism, as well as any distinction between the "immanent" and the "economic" is utterly foreign to Johannine theology' (*The Trinity of Love*, pp. 146–7, n. 11).

and not like anything created and worshiped him as such (see Ex. 33:23; Is. 31:3; Hos. 11:9).[14] There must be more to Jesus' statement that 'God is spirit'.

Hopefully without abusing the text, and in light of the whole Gospel, it would appear to mean that God is Spirit in that the Father is Father and the Son is Son in the Spirit. Christians are to worship the Father in spirit (in the Spirit of truth) and in truth (in the Word of truth conformed by the Spirit of truth) because they too have been conformed by the Spirit into true sons and daughters, and so the Father, in the Spirit, has become their father. Christians, having been conformed by the Spirit into sons, are inserted into the very life of the Trinity where, by the same Spirit, the Father is Father and the Son is Son.

A similar pattern and argument can be discerned in the statement that 'God is love'. If the Spirit is the love in whom the Father begets the Son and so conforms himself as Father and conforms the Son as Son, then to say 'God is love' is not a statement about God's generic nature, but specifies the very heart of the trinitarian life and designates that it is the Spirit that makes the life of God trinitarian. Love (the Spirit) is what makes the Father the Father for it is in love that he begets the Son and it is love (the Spirit) that makes the Son the Son for it is in the Spirit, in whom he is begotten, that he loves the Father.[15]

---

[14] The Old Testament admonition against making an idol or image of Yahweh is founded upon his spiritual ineffable nature. Being spirit, God cannot be imaged (see Ex. 20:3–6; Dt. 5:7–10).

[15] Kasper, while he does not specify the active role of the Spirit as I have, nonetheless states: 'The confession of God as the Father of Jesus Christ is thus in John's view the properly and specifically Christian element, which he puts into words by saying: "God is love"' (*The God of Jesus Christ*, p. 144; cf. p. 155). Also, 'For whom is this love which is God himself?... Must we not rather say that God is love within himself?... Is God not only Father of the world and of human beings but first of all Father of his eternal consubstantial Son? Thus the definition of God's essence as perfect freedom in love turns us back, as does the biblical image of God

Conclusion: Trinitarian Formulae and Doxologies

By way of conclusion, let us take a brief look at a few of the trinitarian formulae and doxologies within the New Testament.[16] These formulae and doxologies, while they do not notably further the thesis, certainly do not count against it.

The baptismal formula in Matthew 28:19, for example, supports the unity and equality of the persons as well as specifying a definite order – the Father, the Son, and the Holy Spirit. While this order gives first place to the Father, I will argue in the next chapter that it is one of source and origin and not one of sequential priority. Even though the formula does not overtly suggest the present thesis, yet the New Testament baptismal theology which developed from this formula, as we saw in Chapter Two, is a constituent component of my argument.

The doxology at the close of the Second Letter to the Corinthians does lend some support for the trinitarian pattern discerned in the New Testament. 'The grace of the Lord Jesus Christ and the love of God' are founded upon 'the fellowship of the Holy Spirit' (2 Cor. 13:14). Through fellowship in the Spirit we share in the Spirit's grace given to us in Christ, and in the Father's love also given to us in the Spirit (see Rom. 5:5). Thus we are incorporated into the life of the Trinity as the Trinity itself exists – the grace and

---

as Father, to the christological ground for the way the Bible talks about God' (ibid., 157).

Kelly writes in a similar vein: 'Love is not a quality that God has or an attitude that the divine three cultivate: it is what God *is* … By equating "God is love" with "God is Trinity", we escape the implication that Love is merely a mode of the divine being, that the reality of God could have been otherwise' (*The Trinity of Love*, p. 178).

See also Wolfhart Pannenberg, *Systematic Theology*, Vol. 1 (Grand Rapids, MI: Eerdmans, 1991), pp. 422–32; Zizioulas, *Being As Communion*, p. 46.

[16] I will only examine Mt 28:19; 2 Cor. 13:14; and 1 Pet. 1:2. For other doxologies in the New Testament see 1 Cor. 12:4–6; Eph. 4:4–6; 2 Thes. 2:13–14 and Rev. 1:4–5.

love between the Father and the Son is in the fellowship of the Spirit for it is through the Spirit that the Father and Son exist for one another.

Similarly, 1 Peter 1:2 proclaims that we were 'chosen and destined by God the Father and sanctified by the Spirit into (*eis*) obedience and into the sprinkling of blood of Jesus Christ' [author's translation]. Through the Spirit's sanctification we are incorporated into the obedience of Jesus, as sons in the Son, by being cleansed of sin through his blood (sanctified into the blood of Jesus). Thus in the Spirit we live out our destiny as being chosen by the Father. As the Spirit conforms us into obedient sons and daughters in Christ, so the Spirit eternally conforms Jesus as the obedient Son even to the shedding of his blood as man.[17]

Even if one might argue with some particulars of the above New Testament exegesis, I believe I have sufficiently demonstrated that there is a specific trinitarian pattern within the New Testament. I have argued that the actions of and roles played by the Father, the Son, and the Holy Spirit in the economy of salvation, expressed principally in functional language, illustrate the actions and roles they play within the immanent Trinity, namely that the Father begets the Son in or by the Holy Spirit, and thus that the Spirit proceeds from the Father as the one in whom the Son is begotten.

---

[17] I will examine 1 Cor. 12:4–6 on the gifts and services being of the same Spirit, the same Lord, and the same God in Chapter Six.

CHAPTER FOUR:

A NEW TRINITARIAN ONTOLOGY

Here I wish to build a metaphysical or systematic understanding of the immanent Trinity on the basis of the New Testament evidence and the received trinitarian traditions of the East and the West, both of which are founded upon the Councils of Nicea (325) and Constantinople (381).

Origin and Action: The Father

Both East and West agree that the distinction of the persons within the Trinity is ordered upon action and origin. From these are established the mutual relations by which the persons of the Trinity subsist and are distinguished.[1]

---

[1]   See Thomas Aquinas, *S.T.*, I, 28, 4; I, 29, 4; I, 36, 2, ad 7; I, 40, 2; I, 40, 4. Aquinas states: 'Now the divine persons are multiplied by reason of their origin: and origin includes the idea of someone from whom another comes, and of someone that comes from another, and by these two modes a person can be known' (ibid., I, 32, 3). Or again: 'In the divine persons distinction is founded on origin. But origin can be properly designated only by certain acts. Wherefore, to signify the order of origin in the divine persons, we must attribute notional acts to the persons' (ibid., I, 41, 1).

   See also Gregory of Nyssa, *Quod non sint tres*; Gregory of Nazianzus, *Or.* 29, 2 and 31, 8–9.

Emulating the scriptural proclamation that the Father is the Father because he is the unbegotten or ingenerate source of the Son and the Holy Spirit, the Orthodox and the Latins ascribe paternity to the Father, for he begets the Son and spirates (breathes forth) the Spirit.[2] What is the precise nature of the Father's paternity? In the conflicting answers to this question lies the real origin of the estrangement between the East and the West. The East suspects that the West in the *filioque* has undermined the monarchy of the Father since the Holy Spirit is also said to proceed from the Son. Orthodox theologians and others argue as well that the *filioque* has subverted the trinitarian nature of God and has accorded priority to the oneness of God, even to the extent of holding that some common single nature or *ousia* supports a trinity of persons which then only embellishes it. The West, in turn, believes that the East has jeopardized the equality and unity of the divine persons, as well as providing insufficient definition to the nature of the Spirit's procession. I believe that the concerns of each are genuine, but I also believe that each has often argued for their respective positions in an improper manner.

The East, in strongly defending the monarchy of the Father, has emphasized that the whole of the Son's and the Spirit's deity find their source in him alone. He not only fashions them as distinct persons, but he also constitutes them as equally God as he is God. The Father is then the *fons divinitatis*. This is true and must be unconditionally preserved.

However, what the East has also done, in wishing to maintain the monarchy of the Father, is to place the entire Godhead in the Father alone. To be God is fundamentally to be the Father. The one nature of God is ultimately that of the Father, and the Son and the Holy Spirit are only derivatively God in that they sequentially obtain their deity from him and so share in *his* Godhead.

---

[2]   See Aquinas, *S.T.*, I, 34.

The difficulty here is one not of preserving the monarchy of the Father, but of affirming that the one God is a Trinity of equal persons. Because the Father alone possesses the Godhead, which he shares with the Son and the Holy Spirit, making them *homoousios* with himself, this position always tends, despite the sincere disclaimers, to undermine the unity of the Godhead and the equality of the Son and the Holy Spirit to the Father. *Homoousios* always tends to become *homoiousios*.[3] This predicament arises because Neo-Platonic emanationism persists within the Eastern view of the Trinity. The Father, not the Trinity, is the *ousia* or being of God from which, in Platonic fashion, the Son and the Holy Spirit emanate.[4]

---

[3]   W. Hill writes: 'The deepest instincts of the Cappadocians are with the *homoiousion* formula, with its corresponding emphasis upon the plurality within the Godhead' (*The Three-Personed God*, p. 47).

[4]   Because of their Neo-Platonic background, W. Hill holds that the Cappadocians believe too readily that 'only the Father is divine by essence. The Son and the Spirit are apt to be thought of as divine in virtue of their unique rapport to their Source ... this is tantamount to saying they are divine in a participatory way (ibid., p. 279–80.)

Pannenberg also writes concerning Basil and the Cappadocians:

> The idea of the Father as the source and origin of deity so fused the person of the Father and the substance of the Godhead that the divine substance is originally proper to the Father alone, being received from him by the Son and Spirit. In distinction from Athanasius this means a relapse into subordinationism, since the idea of the mutual defining of the distinctiveness of the persons does not lead to the thought of an equally mutual ontological constitution of their personhood but is interpreted in terms of relations of origin, of which it can be said that strictly they are constitutive only of the personhood of the Son and Spirit if the Father is the source and origin of deity. ... If the Father, unlike the Son and Spirit, were to be equated with the divine substance, then the Son and Spirit would necessarily be hypostases that are subordinate to the supreme God (*Systematic Theology*, Vol. 1, pp. 280, 283).

See also Boff, *Trinity and Society*, p. 83; and Torrance, *Theological Dialogue Between Orthodox and Reformed Churches*, Vol. 2, pp. 33–4.

To correct this defect, the monarchy of the Father must be established and maintained within the one being of the Trinity and not prior to or outside of it. A more faithful view of Nicea's *homoousion* doctrine, as Athanasius realized, is to conceive the one being of God as the Father who, from within the *homoousios*, begets the Son and spirates the Spirit and so establishes them both in their personhood and in their deity.[5] The one being of God is the Father giving the whole of his divinity to the Son and to the Holy Spirit. This is ultimately what the Orthodox, I believe, rightly wish to proclaim and preserve.

It is in order to preserve the unity and equality of the divine persons that the West has championed the *filioque*. However, as has been stated so often, where the East starts with the persons of the Trinity, and specifically the Father, the West has started with the oneness of God and proceeded to establish the Trinity. This has often given the impression, or is perceived to do so, that there is an underlying nature or substance (an *ousia*) that is prior to and undergirds the three persons. God is not so much a trinity of persons, but a solitary being over which is laid the persons. In this Western conception of the Trinity we find again a Platonic or Aristotelian understanding of God. God is ultimately one substance or nature and not a trinity of persons.

While there is some merit in the customary distinction that the West begins with the unity of God and proceeds to the three persons and that the East begins with the three persons and proceeds to the unity, I think that this distinction is simplistic and not entirely accurate historically.[6]

---

[5]   For a further exposition of and references to Athanasius' insight see the Introduction, n. 26.

[6]   E. Hill believes that this stereotyped distinction is so filled with exceptions that it 'ought simply to be thrown into the theological dustbin' (*The Mystery of the Trinity*, p. 115; see also pp. 116–17, 148–9). See also de Margerie, *The Christian Trinity in History*, pp. 162–3.

Firstly, we must remember that God first revealed himself to be one and not three. Thus the East and the West historically attempted, from the beginning of Patristic thought, to give an account of how the one God could be three and not how three ('persons') could be one God. From the Apologists to the Council of Nicea, the starting point was always the oneness of God, with the subsequent attempt to reconcile the New Testament proclamation of the Father, the Son and the Holy Spirit. Only after Nicea does one find a different emphasis, but the divergence was not merely between the East and the West. Athanasius, for example, grasped that the distinction of persons must be made within the oneness of being. This he believed to be in conformity with the *homoousion* doctrine of Nicea. It is only with the Cappadocians and the later Orthodox Doctors in contrast to the later Latin Doctors (Augustine and Aquinas) that a distinction can be made. However, the distinction is not primarily that the East now stressed the three persons and the West the unity of nature. Rather the real dissimilarity is that the Orthodox begin with the monarchy of the Father from whom the Son and the Holy Spirit proceed. The Father is the ultimate source both of the unity and of the dynamic going forth of the Son and the Holy Spirit.[7] Thus, for the East, the persons of the Trinity assumed a more appealing and energetic character, especially within the economy of salvation.[8] The West, moreover, did not primarily start with the oneness of nature, but rather aspired to conceive how the three persons could nonetheless be one God.[9] This was the heart of Augustine's trinitarian analogies founded upon the human mind.

---

[7]   Gaybba writes: 'The East believed that the unity of the Godhead could only be maintained by affirming the Father to be the sole source of the other persons' (*The Spirit of Love*, p. 126).

[8]   See Kasper, *The God of Jesus Christ*, pp. 259, 296.

[9]   See ibid., pp. 296–8. Kasper states:

The difference between the two approaches (East and West) can also be brought out with the help of images. The line is a suitable image for the Greek conception: the Father begets the Son, and through the Son the Holy Spirit proceeds from him. In the procession of the Spirit the life process in the Trinity reaches its completion, while at the same time in

Secondly, while Augustine's notion of the three persons within the Trinity and their existing as relations remains primarily on a psychological level and not on the level of ontology, yet he was attempting to demonstrate how one being could actually *exist* in three different manners. While Augustine is often accused of giving priority to the oneness of God, it must be remembered that his analogies were formulated precisely to demonstrate how *three* could be one. At the outset of *De Trinitate* he considers that his task is to demonstrate how 'the Father and the Son and the Holy Spirit are of one and the same substance or essence'; or how, according to scripture, the 'Father and Son and Holy Spirit in the inseparable equality of one substance present a divine unity; and therefore there are not three gods but one God.'[10] Augustine's concern is not how one can be three, but rather how three can be one. Faith demands that the 'Father and Son and Holy Spirit are one being. Nor with them is to be anything else than to be God. So Father and Son and Holy Spirit are one God.'[11] The Western

───────────────

the Spirit it also presses out beyond itself. A triangle or a circle is a more suitable image for the Latin conception: the Father begets the Son; the circle of trinitarian life is then closed in the Spirit as the reciprocal love between Father and Son. The Greek conception is thus more open to the world, while the Latin is more self-enclosed (pp. 296–7).

See also LaCugna, *God For Us*, pp. 96–7.

I would somewhat disagree with Kasper's last statement. For the East the Father, through the Son and the Holy Spirit, does reach out to embrace human beings. There is nothing essentially wrong with this unless it is interpreted in a Palamite, and thus Neo-Platonic, sense where God reaches out to us through the divine energies. In which case we are no longer embraced by or related to God as he is in himself, but in some lesser mediatory manner (cf. LaCugna, ibid., pp. 181–205). For the West, while the conception of the Trinity is more self-enclosed, yet through the economy of salvation and the work of grace human beings are incorporated into the very life of the Trinity as it exists in itself and thus share in its inner dynamism. Simply put, for the East the Trinity reaches out to us in a linear fashion, and in the West the Trinity affiliates us to and enfolds us within the circle of its inner life. I will examine this more closely in Chapter Six.

[10]   *The Trinity* I: 2, 7, trans. E. Hill, p. 69.

[11]   Ibid., VII: 6. Boff writes: 'For Augustine, God, in the absolute sense, is not the Father, as for the majority of Eastern theologians, but the Trinity, Father,

stereotype is really only found in Anselm. He does not conceive the persons of the Trinity arising out of the paternity of the Father who begets the Son and spirates the Spirit, but out of the fecundity of their common essence or nature.[12]

Thirdly, Aquinas himself is very clear that the inter-relationship of the persons is what the one God is. He states:

> In God essence is not really distinct from person; and yet ... the persons are really distinguished from each other. For person, signifies relation as subsisting in the divine nature. But relation as referred to the essence does not differ therefrom really, but only in our way of thinking; while as referred to an opposite relation, it has a real distinction by virtue of that oppostion. Thus there are one essence and three persons.[13]

For Aquinas the distinction between essence and persons in God is only due to our way of thinking. In God they are identical. Thus the one nature or being of God is the inter-relationship of the persons. 'We speak of one essence of the three persons, and three persons of the one essence.'[14]

Son and Holy Spirit. His work is full of expressions such as: "The Trinity is the only true God" [De Trinitate, I: 6, 10, 11] or "God is the Trinity" [ibid. VII: 6, 12; XV: 4, 6]' (Trinity and Society, p. 55).

[12] See Monologion, 26–64 and De Processione Spiritus Sancti. For a study of Anselm's trinitarian theology see J. Hopkins, A Companion to the Study of St. Anselm (Minneapolis: University of Minnesota Press, 1972), pp. 90–121. See also Pannenberg, Systematic Theology, Vol. 1, pp. 285–6; and de Margerie, The Christian Trinity in History, p. 316. As we will see shortly, Aquinas does not perceive the one nature of God as distinct from the Trinity.

[13] S.T., I, 39, 1.

[14] Ibid., I, 39, 2; cf. I, 28, 3, ad 1. Today Aquinas is often criticized for beginning the Summa with De Deo Uno and then, only after speaking about the oneness of God, treating De Deo Trino. (See for example: Forte, The Trinity as History, p. 5; LaCugna, God For Us, pp. 6, 44, 145–50; Rahner, The Trinity, 10–21; Zizioulas, Being As Communion, p. 40). Again I believe too much is made of this, as if Aquinas considered the Trinity only as an afterthought. This is not the case. The division

Nonetheless, the dilemma for the West can be similar to that for the East. Instead of conceiving the Godhead as residing in the Father alone as does the East, the West can incline to regard the one Godhead as distinct from the three persons. Neither then locates the Godhead in its proper setting. The Godhead is neither in the Father alone nor is it a solitary substance distinct from the Trinity. The Godhead is the Trinity. The one Godhead, the one being of God, is the action of the Father begetting the Son and spirating the Spirit, and so sharing with them the whole of his deity, constituting them as equal divine persons. Thus the monarchy of the Father is maintained, but within the one being of God who is a trinity of persons.[15]

---

between *De Deo Uno* and *De Deo Trino* was fundamentally pedagogical. Only after the student learned what was 'easy' from reason, could he then take up the more difficult questions involving revelation. Moreover, I suspect that Aquinas was also instinctively following the method of revelation itself. God first revealed himself to be one and only later revealed himself as a trinity of persons.

Equally, the criticism that Aquinas, in *De Deo Trino*, separated *theologia* (God in himself) from *oikonomia* (God for us) is not entirely accurate (LaCugna lists six reasons, gathered from various theologians, why the relationship between *theologia* and *oikonomia* is problematic for Aquinas (*God For Us*, pp. 145–9). It is true that in *De Deo Trino* Aquinas is primarily concerned with the Trinity *in se*, but his very first *quaestio* demonstrates that the processions within God are founded upon the missions (revelation) in the economy and he concludes his treatment of the Trinity by examining the missions of the divine persons (see *S.T.*, I, 27, 1; I, 43). While LaCugna notes this, she fails to give full significance to the fact that, for Aquinas, the whole discussion of the immanent Trinity is bracketed, and thus sustained, within the economy.

The real weakness within Aquinas' structure and method is that he never adequately demonstrated the relationship between God as *ipsum esse* and *actus purus* (I AM WHO AM), and the Trinity. W. Hill has admirably confirmed their inherent relationship. See *The Three-Personed God*, pp. 259–62.

[15] The 1991 agreed statement between the Orthodox and the Reformed Churches stated that the monarchy of the Father must be seen as residing within the whole of the Godhead and not residing within the Father alone apart from the Son and the Holy Spirit. See *Theological Dialogue Between Orthodox and Reformed Churches*, Vol. 2, pp. 223–4, 231.

John Zizioulas and Colin Gunton have forcefully argued that a true understanding of the Christian notion of God must reside in the notion of 'person' and not in the notion of 'substance'. God as a person is what distinguished the Christian understanding of God from that of the Greek philosophers. Gunton believes that the contemporary Western crisis of faith in God is to be laid at the door of Augustine, who, he argues, did not found his notion of the Trinity on the persons, but on the oneness of substance, and so undermines God's trinitarian and thus personal relationship to the world in creation and redemption. 'The only conclusion can be that, in some sense or other, it is divine substance and not the Father that is the basis of the being of God, and therefore, *a fortiori*, of everything else.'[16]

Zizioulas argues that if the ontology of God consists in the substance of God, then

> This would bring us back to the ancient Greek ontology: God first *is* God (His substance or nature, His being), and then exists as Trinity, that is as persons. This interpretation in fact prevailed in Western theology and unfortunately entered into modern Orthodox dogmatics with the arrangement in the dogmatic handbooks of the headings 'On the One God' followed by 'On the Trinity.' The significance of this interpretation lies in the assumption that the ontological 'principle' of God is not found in the person but in the substance, that is, in the 'being' itself of God. Indeed the idea took shape in Western theology that that which constitutes the unity of God is the one divine substance, the one divinity; this is, as it were, the ontological 'principle' of God.[17]

Zizioulas, and in a similar fashion Gunton also, argues that there must be a return to the insight of the Cappadocians:

> Among the Greek Fathers the unity of God, the one God, and the ontological 'principle' or 'cause' of the being and life of God does not consist in the one substance of God but in the *hypostasis*,

---

[16] Gunton, *The Promise of Trinitarian Theology*, p. 54; see also pp. 31–57; see also *The One, the Three and the Many*, pp. 188–95.

[17] Zizioulas, *Being As Communion*, p. 40.

that is, *the person of the Father*. The one God is not the one substance but the Father, who is the 'cause' both of the generation of the Son and of the procession of the Spirit ... And the one divine substance is consequently the being of God only because it has these three modes of existence, which it owes not to the substance but to one person, the Father. Outside the Trinity there is no God, that is no divine substance, because the ontological 'principle' of God is the Father.[18]

While I believe both Gunton and Zizioulas are a little harsh on Augustine and the Western tradition (Anselm is more the culprit than Augustine), I nonetheless wholeheartedly support their desire to found the Christian understanding of God on the notion of 'person' and not on that of 'substance'.[19] Moreover, what the West needs to learn from the East is

---

[18] Ibid., pp. 40–41. Zizioulas also writes with regard to the Cappadocian notion of person:

> For the first time in the history of philosophy, particularly of Greek thought, we have an identification of an ontological category, such as *hypostasis*, with a notion such as Person ... By calling Person a 'Mode of being' (*tropos hyparxeos*) the Cappadocians introduced a revolution into Greek ontology, since they said for the first time in history that a) a *prosopon*, is not secondary to being, but its *hypostasis;* b) a *hypostasis*, i.e. an ontological category, is relational in its very nature, it is *prosopon*. The importance of this lies in the fact that Person is now the *ultimate* ontological category we can apply to God. Substance is not something ontologically prior to Person (no classical Greek would say this), but its real existence is to be found in the Person ('The Teaching of the 2nd Ecumenical Council on the Holy Spirit in Historical and Ecumenical Perspective', in *Credo In Spiritum Sanctum*, Vol. 1, pp. 35–6).

See also J.D. Zizioulas, 'On Being a Person. Towards an Ontology of Personhood', in *Persons, Divine and Human. King's College Essays in Theological Anthropology*, Christoph Schwöbel and Colin Gunton (eds) (Edinburgh: T&T Clark, 1992); Gunton, *The Promise of Trinitarian Theology*, pp. 35–42.

[19] W. Hill correctly notes that Aquinas moves beyond the psychological notions of Augustine and establishes the ontological status of persons of the Trinity.

Aquinas deliberately attempts a transition beyond the psychological

that the notion of personhood is inherently dynamic. The Father must be the dynamic source and fount of the Son and the Holy Spirit. The Son and the Holy Spirit, in their respective personhoods, must equally be in a dynamic relationship with the Father. (It is in this latter respect that I believe both the East and the West are seriously inadequate in their conceptions.) However, I believe that, in attempting to free the Trinity from the tar pit of 'substance', Gunton and Zizioulas have now immersed the Father in it. In trying to preserve the personhood of God on the basis of the monarchy of the Father, they have ensnared themselves in Neo-Platonic emanationism, the very Greek philosophy from which they wish to be liberated. 'The one God' is now '*the person of the Father*'. If the one God is the Father, then by necessity, the Son and the Holy Spirit are not one in being, *homoousios*, with the Father . To say that they are *homoousios* with the

---

processes of the soul to its very beingness. The resultant relationality is an ontological one, grounded in being itself as a dynamism and not merely a self-referencing achieved by way of the soul's activity. The knowing and naming of God moves in the same direction as it did for Augustine, namely, from revelation about God to the perceiving of analogies in the soul. But behind the notion of God as Trinity lies the notion of God as the Pure Act of Being, wherein 'to be,' 'to know,' and 'to love' coincide in the absolute self-identity (*The Three-Personed God*, p. 70; cf. p. 72).

Unlike Augustine's notion of person, Aquinas' is 'profoundly metaphysical' (ibid., p. 64).

Thus Aquinas identifies the nature and persons of God and does not see them as separate in reality. 'The divine processions are in the identity of the same nature' (*S.T.*, I, 28, 1). 'Relations really existing in God have the existence of the divine essence in no way distinct therefrom ... Thus it is clear that in God relation and essence do not differ from each other, but are one and the same' (ibid., I, 28, 2). 'For person, signifies relation as subsisting in the divine nature. But relation as referred to the essence does not differ therefrom really, but only in our way of thinking; while as referred to an opposite relation, it has a real distinction by virtue of that opposition. Thus there are one essence and three persons' (ibid., I, 39, 1; see also I, 29, 4; I, 40, 2).

W. Hill states: 'The relations in God then are not "in relation to" the divine nature at all (except in the abstractions of finite thought); rather they bespeak simple identity therewith. Each subsisting relation *is* God and all three of them together *are* God' (*The Three-Personed God*, p. 266; see also p. 267).

Father would mean either that they emanate out from him and so share the same divine substance in a generic sense which would make for three gods (which is why Arius denied the *homoousios* and why Eusebius stressed that Nicea only wanted to uphold the true divinity of the Son and not that there are three gods), or else that the Son and the Holy Spirit are the Father, which is Sabellianism (which is what the Homoiousians feared, including Basil). What one needs to grasp is that the whole oneness of God's being (the *homoousios*) is itself a trinity of persons.

The person of the Father indeed constitutes the ontological being and personhood of the Son and the Holy Spirit, but he does so in the one being of God.[20] The substance of God is not the Father. The being of God (I prefer the expression 'the being of God' to the phrase 'the substance of God') *is* the Trinity which is the one act of the Father begetting the Son and spirating the Spirit. The eternal constituting of the persons takes place within (and not outside of) the one being of God, and therefore is the one being of God. There is neither a priority of oneness nor of threeness. Three persons *are* one God or one God *is* three persons.[21]

---

[20]   Aquinas clearly maintains that 'the Father in begetting the Son does not transmit any part of his nature, but communicates his whole nature to him, the distinction only of origin remaining, as explained above (I, 40, 2)' (*S.T.*, I, 41, 3; see also I, 33, 1; I, 39, 5; I, 42, 5). LaCugna is correct in saying that Aquinas corrects Augustine by 'making person absolute' (*God For Us*, p. 174, n. 57).

[21]   What W. Hill writes is pertinent to all of the above.

At bottom, Aquinas's trinitarianism is a variation on Augustine's focal concept of relational unity. Augustine's own thought suffered the limitation of emasculating 'person' of any real import when said of God in the plural ... However, this represents a deliberate option on the part of Thomas. In making it, he is rejecting the Dionysian schema whose *point de départ* is the notion of the First Person in God as '*fons divinitatis.*' This allows Pseudo-Dionysius to view the Father as person in a way not readily extended to the *Logos* and the *Pneuma*. The deepest instinct in such thought is Neo-Platonic; the Trinity is explained on the basis of emanations from the Father who is acknowledged to be God prior (conceptually) to his giving origin to Son and Spirit. Unity in God is then explained by a 'reduction' of the Second and the Third Persons to their Unoriginate Source. The unity is hierarchical rather than purely

I have argued at length for a proper understanding of the monarchy of the Father for only if he is rightly placed within the Trinity will the Trinity itself assume its precise and true configuration. And, as I will argue shortly, this monarchy of the Father as well as the unity of the Trinity will only be rightly understood if an appropriate active role is given to the Holy Spirit. Let us proceed then to examine the roles of the Son and the Holy Spirit within the Trinity.

Origin and Action: The Son

The Son is the Son because he is begotten from the Father and proceeds from the Father by way of generation. Filiation is ascribed then to the Son. This designation of the Father as Father and of the Son as Son is founded principally upon the revelation of Jesus, that he is the incarnate Son of the Father. On the basis of an understanding of human begetting, analogous content can be derived in applying the terms 'generation', when applied to the Father begetting the Son, and to 'filiation', when applied to the Son as begotten.[22] The Son eternally comes forth from the Father as the Father's perfect image and offspring.[23] The Son being designated Word also furthers this understanding. As the human intellect conceives a mental word, so analogously does the Father conceive his perfect Word.[24] Each of

---

relational – a mode of thinking betrayed in the very title of the writings of Pseudo-Dionysius: *De hierarchia*. This approach enjoyed an ascendancy in the Eastern tradition.

While such a view can speak admirably of the work of the Son and the Spirit within the mystery of salvation, Hill concludes that it is nonetheless 'crypto-subordinationism' (*The Three-Personed God*, pp. 77–8). See also Boff, *Trinity and Society*, pp. 145–7.

[22] See Aquinas, *S.T.*, I, 27, 2; I, 28, 4; I, 41.

[23] See ibid., I, 35.

[24] See ibid., I, 34.

the terms, 'Father' and 'Son', presupposes the other and the relationship between them. The Father would not be Father unless he had a Son, and the Son would not be Son unless he had a Father.[25] We have emphasized thus far that the Son is Son because he is begotten from the Father. This is purely passive in nature. Is there a reciprocal act that the Son performs which equally constitutes his being the Son in relationship to the Father and so, in some sense, constitutes the Father as Father? This question can only be answered in light of the role of the Holy Spirit.

Origin and Action: The Holy Spirit

The early Church labored over what differentiated the Holy Spirit from the Son. Why was the Spirit not a second Son or a Grandson?[26] What differentiated the proceeding of the Holy Spirit from that of the Son? If the Spirit was not begotten, what was the nature of his procession?

While both East and West struggled to find an answer and ultimately appealed to mystery, they at least attempted to give some content to the nature of the Spirit's procession.[27]

---

[25] Augustine writes: 'Since the Father is only called so because he has a Son, and the Son is only called so because he has a Father, these things are not said substance-wise, as neither is said with reference to itself but only with reference to the other' (De Trinitate, V:6). For Augustine the Father's 'very "is" has reference not to himself but to the Son' (ibid., VII:2).

[26] It is interesting that the question of whether or not the Holy Spirit is a Grandson arises only out of a mind-set formed on Neo-Platonic emanationism. The Spirit proceeds from Father through the Son and therefore might be called a Grandson.

[27] For example, Gregory of Nazianzus asks his critics in frustration:

What, then, is procession? Do you tell me what is the unbegottenness of the Father, and I will explain to you the physiology of the generation of the Son and the process of the Spirit, and we shall both of us be frenzy-stricken for prying into the mystery of God. And who are we to do these

The East has emphasized that the Spirit, while proceeding from the Father alone, proceeds through the Son and so is distinguished from the Son.[28] The West has maintained that the Spirit proceeds principally from the Father as the Love of the Father for the Son and so proceeds equally, but derivatively, from the Son as the Son's Love

things, we who cannot even see what lies at our feet, or number the sands of the sea, or the drops of rain, or the days of eternity, much less enter into the depths of God, and supply an account of that nature which is so unspeakable and transcending all words? (*Or.*, 31, 8).

While the mystery of the Trinity cannot be fully grasped by the human mind, it would be wrong to think that we cannot come to any knowledge of it. Thus to say, as Tityu Koev does, that the distinction between the 'begetting' of the Son and the 'proceeding' of the Holy Spirit 'is a mystery of the Divine Life, which is completely beyond the human mind' ('The Doctrine of the Holy Trinity on the Basis of the Nicene-Constantinopolitan Symbol of Faith', *Theological Dialogue Between Orthodox and Reformed Churches*, Vol. 2, p. 70) does injustice both to man and to God since God must have thought we could, in some incomplete but fruitful manner, grasp it in that it was he himself who revealed it to us. To be in complete ignorance about this distinction does not lead to holy wonder and awe, but to complete intellectual frustration.

[28] For a discussion of the procession of the Holy Spirit in Patristic Orthodox thought see the classic work of H.B. Swete, *The Holy Spirit in the Ancient Church* (London: Macmillan, 1912), especially pp. 230–54. See also Hanson's excellent summary in *The Search for the Christian Doctrine of God*, pp. 738–90, J. Pelikan, *The Christian Tradition: A History of the Development of Doctrine*, Vol. 1: *The Emergence of the Catholic Tradition (100–600)* (Chicago: University Press, 1971), pp. 211–25. For a survey of later Eastern development see Pelikan, *The Christian Tradition: A History of the Development of Doctrine*, Vol. 2: *The Spirit of Eastern Christendom (600–1700)* (Chicago: University Press, 1974), pp. 170–98.

It should be noted that prior to the Photian controversy the East did not stress that the Spirit proceeded solely from the Father, but used the customary expression 'through the Son'. Thus Fahey writes that at this time 'Photius himself introduced an element that seems in the judgement of many scholars not only in the West to be innovative. For Photius stated that the true patristic principle about the Holy Spirit is that the Spirit proceeds from the *Father alone* (*ek* monou *Patros ekporeuetai*)' ('Son and Spirit: Divergent Theologies Between Constantinople and the West', *Concilium: Conflicts About the Holy Spirit* 128 (8/1979) 21).

for the Father.[29]

While I believe that the West has given more precise definition
to the notion of the Spirit's procession, and thus to why the Spirit is

---

[29] LaCugna states that Augustine is 'the first to call the Holy Spirit Love:
Love of Father and Son for each other' (*God For Us*, p. 90). See Augustine, *De
Trinitate*, V:12, 13; VI:5, 7; VII:3, 6; XV:17, 27, 30–1, 37, 47–8. See also Aquinas,
S.T., I, 36.
    The work of Jean-Miguel Garrigues should be noted here. Garrigues has
pointed out that the English word 'proceed' is used to translate both the Greek
word *ekporeuesthai* and the Latin word *procedere*. Yet these two words historically
have significantly different nuances that have been, and often continue to be,
unappreciated and unknown.
    Ekporeuomai in the middle voice implies the subject in action and thus signifies
'to pass' or 'to go across'.

    The Greek form of the Nicene Creed, *ek tou Patros ekporeuomenon*, would
    not therefore have been translated by *qui ex patre procedit* but, more exactly,
    by *qui ex patre se exportat*, which might be rendered in French by 'qui se
    porte hors du Père', 'qui sort du Père', in English perhaps 'who goes
    forth out of the Father'; 'who issues from the Father'... If the Greek term
    ekporeusthai as such denotes a passage out of that from which one issues
    in distinction from it, the Latin *procedere* has the inverse connotation.
    Cedere means 'to go from by giving place to', 'to retire'... the form *procedere*
    means to go forward giving place to that from which one moves away
    and to which by that very fact one remains connected ... St Thomas
    Aquinas pointed out that the Latin term *processio* is the most general
    there is to designate any relation of origin. ... In the example he gives,
    what is expressed is not, as in the Greek *ekporeusis*, a passage out of the
    origin which distinguishes what comes out from it, but the progression
    starting from the origin of what moves forward while maintaining with
    it a homogeneous link of communion ...The origin is not apprehended
    first of all as the principle from which a distinction issues but as the
    starting-point of a continuous process ('A Roman Catholic View of the
    Position Now Reached in the Question of the Filioque', *Spirit of God,
    Spirit of Christ*, pp. 158–9).

    See also *L'Esprit Qui Dit 'Père!'*, pp. 57–84. Also see Zizioulas, 'The Teaching
of the 2nd Ecumenical Council, Vol. 1, pp. 48–9.
    In this study I hope to recapture the dynamism of *ekporeuomai* without the
implication that the Spirit goes out from the Father in a linear fashion.

the Spirit and not another Son, yet both the East and West have given inadequate accounts of the Spirit's procession.

The question never fully addressed by either tradition is this: if both the Son and the Spirit proceed from the Father, what is there in the nature of the Father's fatherhood that gives rise to the Spirit without making the Spirit another Son? The West would answer that the Spirit proceeds as the fatherly love for the Son, and the filial love for the Father. Augustine and Aquinas emphasize that as the Son proceeds by way of the intellect, so the Spirit proceeds by way of the will – as the Love of the Father for the known Word.[30] This may be true, but such a view does not probe deep enough.

The deeper reason, which is the thesis of this study, is that the Father is the Father in that he begets the Son in the Spirit. The Father spirates the Spirit in the same act by which he begets the Son, for the Spirit proceeds from the Father as the fatherly Love in whom or by whom the Son is begotten.[31] The very nature then of

---

[30] For references to Augustine see n. 29, and for Aquinas see S.T., I, 27, 3–4.

[31] I agree with Augustine and Aquinas that the proper name of the Holy Spirit is Love or Gift. See Augustine, De Trinitate, XV: 29, 31, 33–6 and Aquinas, S.T., I, 37; I, 38. Most contemporary Latin theologians also see the Holy Spirit as the bond of Love between the Father and the Son. See for example Gaybba, The Spirit of Love, pp. 130–7; Kasper, The God of Jesus Christ, pp. 223–9; Kelly, The Trinity of Love, pp. 139–202; Pannenberg, Systematic Theology, Vol. 1, p. 268.

St Gregory of Palamas was the first Orthodox theologian to designate the Holy Spirit as the love of the Father for the Son (see Markos Orphanos, 'The Procession of the Holy Spirit According to Certain Later Greek Fathers', Spirit of God, Spirit of Christ, p. 33).

Von Balthasar, like Mühlen, sees the Holy Spirit as the 'We' that springs forth from the Love of the 'I-Thou' of the Father and the Son. The Holy Spirit is not only what unites the Father and the Son, but he is also the fruit of their love. He is their common breath. See Explorations in Theology I, p. 169, and Explorations in Theology III, pp. 105–7, 125–7, 151, 156, 355. See also H. Mühlen, Der Heilige Geist als Person (2nd edition) (Münster: Aschendorff, 1967). As the mutual love shared by the Father and the Son the Holy Spirit, for von Balthasar, is also the source and locus of the beauty of God. See Patrick Sherry, *Spirit and Beauty: An Introduction to Theological Aesthetics* (Oxford: Clarendon Press, 1992), pp. 85–109, especially pp. 103–8.

Coffey has long championed what he, until recently, called the 'bestowal model' of the Trinity. Unlike the 'procession model' which sees the Son proceeding from the Father and then the Spirit proceeding from the Father and (or through) the Son, the 'bestowal model' understands that 'the Father bestows his love on the Son generated by him, and the Son in return bestows his love on the Father, this mutual love being the Holy Spirit' *(Grace: The Gift of the Holy Spirit*, p. 11; see also p. 30. See also 'A Proper Mission of the Holy Spirit', 227–50, especially p. 232, and 'The Holy Spirit as the Mutual Love of the Father and the Son', *Theological Studies* 51 (1990) 193–229).

For Coffey the most basic statement that can be made about the Holy Spirit *'is that he is the love with which the Father loves the Son' (Grace: The Gift of the Holy Spirit*, p. 28). However, the love of the Father for the Son does not lie dormant in the Son, but rather with the same love with which he himself is loved the Son loves the Father. 'The Father's love for the Son will precede, and indeed evokes, the Son's love for the Father' ('The "Incarnation" of the Holy Spirit in Christ', p. 472). Thus 'the breathing forth of the Holy Spirit has a purpose in the Trinity, viz. he is breathed forth as the mutual love of the Father and the Son' *(Grace: The Gift of the Holy Spirit*, p. 31). Because he believes that the unique emphasis of the 'bestowal model' is the return of the Son's love for the Father in the Holy Spirit, Coffey prefers now to call his trinitarian theology 'the model of return' ('The Holy Spirit as the Mutual Love of the Father and the Son', p. 228).

Now Coffey verges on the present thesis when he states that the Son proceeds from the Father's love for him. Quoting Mühlen he writes: 'One is entitled to say that the Father produces the Son *ex aliquo amore*, i.e. out of the love with which he wills that the Son together with him produce the Holy Spirit' *(Grace: The Gift of the Holy Spirit*, p. 19). However, because Coffey does not give any active role to the Spirit in the begetting of the Son, he does not fully see that it is in the Father spirating the Spirit that the Son is simultaneously begotten in and by the Spirit; that is, in the love of the Father. The Holy Spirit conforms the Son to be the Son and so allows him to love the Father by the same Spirit (Love) in whom he is begotten.

While Coffey is obviously a strong supporter of the *filioque*, he nonetheless believes that his rejuvenated and nuanced understanding of the Holy Spirit as the mutual love between the Father and the Son is compatible with the concerns of the Orthodox and can actually further the ecumenical dialogue. 'As the *mutual* love for the Father and the Son, the Holy Spirit must be one and must therefore proceed from a single principle, which is here indicated to be the Father and the Son (Western position). But as the love of the Father for the Son (most basic statement), the Holy Spirit must also be said to proceed from the Father alone (Eastern position)' ('A

the Father's paternity demands that he beget the Son in Love and so
the Holy Spirit naturally and necessarily proceeds from him as the
Love in whom the Son is begotten.[32]

While in human beings something must first be known before
it is loved, in God the knowing and loving are simultaneous – the

Proper Mission of the Holy Spirit', p. 249; see also 'The Holy Spirit as the Mutual
Love of the Father and the Son', p. 220).

[32] Durrwell writes:

> The Spirit is not born of the Father, his relationship with the Father is
> different from that of the Son: 'he proceeds from the Father'. However,
> his relationship with the divine sonship is very intimate. He proceeds in
> the begetting of the Son, he is the Spirit of the Father in his fatherhood.
> The entire activity of the Father is to beget the Son, and although God
> does not beget the Spirit, it is nonetheless in his fatherhood that he is
> the source of the Spirit...We must repeat emphatically: the whole mystery
> of the Father is to beget his Son; if therefore the Spirit proceeds from the
> Father whose whole mystery consists in begetting, and if he himself is
> not the Son, *he must therefore be this begetting*. Although human language
> fails us, it would seem that one could say: the Spirit is the action of the
> Father as father, he is the begetting (*The Holy Spirit of God*, pp. 140–1,
> see also pp. 10, 25, 140–55).

I have one caveat to what Durrwell says. I do not want to collapse the
'begetting' and the 'proceeding'. My fear is that to do so would verge on modalism
and also depersonalize the Spirit to a mere process – that of begetting. Therefore, I
am not completely happy with Durrwell saying that the Spirit 'is the begetting'. I
would want to say that the Spirit proceeds from the Father in the begetting of the
Son and that the Son is begotten in or by the Spirit. The begetting and the spirating
are simultaneous but distinct acts of the Father. The Father begets the Son and
conforms him to be Son by the Holy Spirit who proceeds from the Father as the one
in whom the Son is begotten. This distinction may be subtle but, I believe, necessary,
and hopefully clear.

In a similar vein Moltmann writes: 'He (the Holy Spirit) proceeds not only
from the Father, but also from his fatherhood ... The birth of the Son is so intensively
accompanied by the procession of the Spirit from the Father that we have to say:
the Son is begotten by the Father through the Spirit' (*The Spirit of Life*, pp. 306–7).
See also Moltmann, *The Trinity and the Kingdom of God*, p. 184.

begetting and spirating come forth from the Father as distinct, but concurrent, acts. The Father does not, even logically, first beget the Son and then love the Son in the Spirit. The begetting of the Son and the proceeding of the Spirit are simultaneous and, while distinct, mutually inhere in one another. The Father is the Father because, in the one act by which he is eternally constituted as the Father, the Spirit proceeds as the Love (Life and Truth) in whom the Son is begotten of the Father.[33]

This understanding of the procession of the Holy Spirit provides more precise definition to the paternity of the Father, for we now clearly see that the Father is truly the Father not only in begetting

---

[33]   Fahey writes: 'Latin theology following Augustine came to argue that on the level of origin, the generation of the Son precedes the procession of the Holy Spirit' ('Son and Holy Spirit: Divergent Theologies between Constantinople and the West', *Concilium: Conflicts About the Holy Spirit* 128 (8/1979) 18). Commenting on Aquinas, W. Hill states that 'Loving is understood as rooted in a *logically* prior knowing, and knowing is understood as rooted in a *logically* prior beingness' (*The Three-Personed God*, p. 76). My understanding does away with this precedence and 'logical priority'.

Hill, later in the exposition of his own trinitarian conception states:

> It is important to note that the Father is a divine subject who simultaneously (in time and nature) relates himself not only to the Son but also to the *Pneuma*. There is no priority of the Son's origin to that of the Spirit. By the same token, the Father is not *before* the Son and the Spirit as if he were a distinct person antecedently to speaking the Word and spirating the *Pneuma*. There is no succession or priority among the divine persons; to think so is a capitulation to Neo-Platonic emanationism. There is, of course, a real *order* among the trinitarian members – founded in the *logical* order between being-knowing-loving. The intelligibility of love, for example, bespeaks a prior formality which is awareness; moreover, unlike knowledge, it demands as its condition the existence of two persons (ibid., pp. 270–1; see also p. 281).

Even though Hill has overcome Neo-Platonic emanationism, he has not liberated himself from Aristotelian epistemology which demands that, while the Son and Spirit do not proceed in a successive priority, yet they do proceed in logical priority. Logically the Son must 'first' be known 'before' he is loved.

the Son, but he also exercises his paternity in spirating the Spirit as the fatherly love in whom and by whom the Son is begotten. This view of the Trinity also captures the authentic concern of the Orthodox in that it grounds more deeply not only the monarchy of the Father, but also his inherent dynamism. The Father acts truly as the Father as the *fons divinitatis* from whom come both the Son and the Spirit.

Moreover, this view of the Trinity equally confers meaningful distinctness on the nature of the Son's begetting and the Holy Spirit's procession. The Son is Son because, having been begotten by the Father in the Spirit of sonship, he loves the Father as Son. This act of filial love, enacted in the Spirit of sonship, is what makes him the Son. This means that the Father is the Father not only because he begets the Son, but also because, in the begetting of the Son, the Son loves the Father, and so as Son helps constitute the Father as Father. The Father would not be Father unless he had a Son who loved him as Son. Now the cornerstone which holds together this fatherly act of lovingly begetting the Son and this filial act of the Son loving the Father is provided by the action of the Spirit.

The one action by which the Spirit is the Spirit is then twofold in effect – pertaining to the Father and to the Son. The Spirit, springing forth within the Father as his love in or by which the Son is begotten, conforms the Father to be the Father for the Son and concurrently conforms the Son to be the Son for the Father. Putting it more strongly, hopefully not too strongly, it is by the Spirit that the Father substantiates or 'persons' himself as Father because it is by the Spirit that he begets the Son. In so doing the Father substantiates or 'persons', by the same Spirit, the Son and the Son personally re-acts, and so is 'personed' in the Spirit of sonship, as Son of the Father.[34]

---

[34] There are suggestions of the above in von Balthasar. He states that the Son is 'begotten in love' which is the Holy Spirit. He continues:

As the unity of Father and Son, God is one single Spirit: i.e., the love

This does not imply that the Spirit has now taken precedence over the Father and the Son. The order within the Trinity is still maintained. The Father is the unbegotten source of the Son and the Spirit. But the order within the Trinity now completely transcends an emanationist view (Neo-Platonic in origin) which implies not only an order of origin and derivation, but also an order of priority, precedence and sequence, which undermines the eternal nature of the one trinitarian act and thus the divine equality of the persons. While the Spirit 'persons' the Father as Father and the Son as Son, he does so only because he is equally and simultaneously substantiated or 'personed' by the Father and the Son, since it is by proceeding from them that the Spirit becomes the Spirit of the Father and the Son. Thus the Spirit principally proceeds from the Father as the love in which the Father begets the Son and so conforms the Father as Father, and equally, but derivatively, proceeds from the Son as the Spirit who, in conforming the Son as Son, is the Spirit by which the Son loves the Father. The term 'spiration', as designating the nature of the Spirit's proceeding and the role that he plays within the Trinity, here again possesses real definition and specificity.

Before proceeding it may be useful to apply this trinitarian ontology to two biblical images. Firstly, the word 'Abba' contains within it this trinitarian ontology. The term 'Abba' testifies to the monarchy of the Father. The Father is 'Abba' in that he begets the Son, and the Son is Son (what makes him be who he is) by crying out 'Abba!', to the Father. Moreover, this 'Abba', as pertaining to the Father and to the Son, is suffused with the

---

that makes the Father a Father as the one who begets and the love that makes the Son a Son as the Word which expresses him are one single, concrete Spirit-being, and yet the divine Spirit as the 'Third Person' comes forth from this fellowship as the miracle of eternal fruitfulness, not begotten by them both (as is the child by man and woman), but ineffably welling forth from the common 'breath' (*pneuma*) of their mutual indwelling (*Explorations in Theology III: Creator Spirit*, pp. 105–7).

See also *Theo-Drama*, Vol. *III*, pp. 518–19.

Holy Spirit. The Spirit makes this mutual and reciprocal 'Abba'-love to be 'Abba'-love. It is the Spirit who conforms the Father as 'Abba' to the Son and conforms the Son to cry 'Abba!' to the Father. The Spirit makes the Father and the Son be what they are to one another because he proceeds from both as their mutual love for one another.

Clarity may similarly be enhanced by placing all of this in the context of the Father eternally speaking his Word. The Father spirates (breathes forth) the Spirit, and it is in or by the breath of the Spirit that the Father speaks his Word.[35] The Father speaks his eternal Word by the breath of the Holy Spirit, the Spirit of Truth. It is this breath (this spirating of the Spirit), then, which conforms the Father as the Word/Truth-Speaker (the Father), and it is by this same breath that the Word is conformed into the true Word (the Son). The Son in turn breathes forth the Spirit as he cries out 'Abba!' Thus the Holy Spirit is the common breath (life) shared by the Father and the Son.

This image of the Father breathing forth his Word by the breath of the Spirit may be the strongest link the thesis of this book has with the

---

[35] Clément understands the procession of the Spirit in this same manner: 'To say that the Spirit "proceeds" from the Father is necessarily to name the Son, since from all eternity the Father puts his Other in unity; so when he causes the Spirit to "proceed" he remains the Father *of the Son*. To say that the Son is "begotten" of the Father is necessarily to name the Spirit, the Breath that carries the Word' (*The Roots of Christian Mysticism*, p. 72).

Boff also states: 'The Holy Spirit is breathed out by the Father in his Word (Son), since Word (Son) and breath (Spirit) are inseparable' (*Trinity and Society*, p. 140; cf. p. 133).

Similarly, Moltmann writes:

> The inner coherence (within the Trinity) immediately becomes perceptible when we understand the Son as *The Word* (Logos). The Father utters his eternal Word in the eternal breathing out of his Spirit. There is in God no Word without the Spirit, and no Spirit without the Word. In this respect the uttering of the Word and the issuing of the Spirit belong indissolubly together. It is even difficult to perceive that the second Person has any priority over the third Person of the Trinity. Word and Spirit, Spirit and Word issue together and simultaneously from the Father, for they mutually condition one another (*The Trinity and the Kingdom of God*, pp. 169–70).

trinitarian tradition of both the East and the West. Gregory of Nyssa for example states:

> For it would not be right that God's Word should be more defective than our own, which would be the case if, since our word is associated with breath (spirit), we were to believe he lacked a Spirit . . . In the same way, when we learn that God has a Spirit, which accompanies his Word and manifests his activity, we do not think of it as an emission of breath. For we should degrade the majesty of God's power were we to conceive of his Spirit in the same way as ours. On the contrary, we think of it as a power really existing by itself and in its own special subsistence. It is not able to be separated from God in whom it exists, or from God's Word which it accompanies. It is not dissipated into non-existence; but like God's Word it has it own subsistence, is capable of willing, is self-moved and active.[36]

John Damascene, commenting on Gregory, writes: 'When we speak a word, this movement of the air produces the voice, which alone makes the meaning of the word accessible to others.' In an analogous manner, in God too there is a breath, namely, the Spirit 'which accompanies the word and reveals its efficacy'.[37]

Aquinas states that the term 'spirit' can be applied to the Holy Spirit because it implies 'impulse and motion' as do breath and the wind. 'Now it is a property of love to move and impel the will of the lover towards the object loved.'[38] Also the name 'Holy Spirit' suggests a relationship since it

---

[36] *Oratio Catechetica Magna*, 2, trans. from *Christology of the Later Fathers*, ed. E. Hardy (Philadelphia: Westminster Press, 1954). See Basil the Great, *On the Holy Spirit*, XVIII, 46. See also Gaybba, *The Spirit of Love*, pp. 56–7.

[37] *De Fide Orth.* I, 7, as quoted by Kasper, *The God of Jesus Christ*, pp. 216–17. For a similar view see Dragas' comments on Athanasius' theology of the Holy Spirit: 'St Athanasius on the Holy Spirit and the Trinity', *Theological Dialogue Between Orthodox and Reformed Churches*, Vol. 2, pp. 51–4.

[38] *S.T.*, I, 36, 1.

can be understood 'as including a relation, if we understand the Holy Spirit as being breathed (*spiratus*)'.[39]

However, while East and West, through this portrayal of the Spirit as breath, are very close to the present thesis, they never quite saw that the Father breathes forth the Word by the breath of the Spirit. The East never perceived this because their conception of the Trinity is Neo-Platonic, and thus the Spirit ranked third in the hierarchy and so proceeded through the Son. The Spirit then could not be the breath from which the Son was formed. Likewise, the West, in patterning its conception of the Trinity after Aristotelian epistemology, maintained that the Spirit proceeded from the will of the Father as his love for the Son only 'after' the Son was begotten and thus known. So, again, the Spirit here could not be perceived as the breath of the Father in whom the Word is spoken.[40]

---

[39] Ibid., ad 2.

[40] E. Hill has some very telling words on this point:

'Holy Spirit', as we have seen, is only by theological convention a name of relationship. Thomas Aquinas, giving full force to the derivation of the word 'spirit' from *spirare*, 'to breathe', will suggest that we can think of the Holy Spirit as the Breath of God, analogously to the Son's being the Word of God. Strange that Augustine never seems to have thought of this, seeing that a hint to this effect is given in Jn 20:22, where the risen Lord 'breathed on them and said to them, Receive the Holy Spirit'. So the Holy Spirit is the Breath of God, the Father and the Son *together* being the breathers [emphasis added]. He is also the Gift of God, Father and Son together being the giver (*The Mystery of the Trinity*, p. 72).

Because Aquinas has the Word exist logically prior to the Spirit, the Father could never breathe forth the Word in the Spirit. The breathing forth would have to be done together as part of the *filioque*.

Aquinas was ever so close to the present thesis when he stated that, similar to the will, the Spirit proceeds 'by way of impulse and movement towards an object ... So what proceeds in God by way of love ... proceeds rather as spirit; which name expresses a certain vital movement and impulse, accordingly as anyone is described as moved or impelled by love *to perform an action* [emphasis added]' (*S.T.*, I, 27, 4).

Now if Aquinas had recognized that the Father by love (by the Spirit) was impelled to perform that action by which the Son is begotten, he would have

Perichoresis of Action

To proceed then, what we have found here is a mutual co-inherence or *perichoresis* of *action* within the Trinity which makes the persons be who they distinctively are.[41] While the Son and the Holy Spirit come forth from the Father, yet in the coming forth all three persons

---

perceived that the Father begets the Son in the Spirit. However, his Aristotelian epistemology obstructed him from ever considering this possibility. The object (the Son) must first be present before a person (the Father) through the impulse or movement of will (the Spirit) could love it (the Son).

For studies of 'breath' in relation to the Holy Spirit see H. Adams, 'Biblical Images of the Holy Spirit Interpreted in the Light of the Fathers of the Church', *Credo In Spiritum Sanctum*, Vol. 1, pp. 266–9; and de Margerie, *The Christian Trinity in History*, pp. 24–32.

[41] The term *perichoresis* first entered the theological vocabulary on the Christological level. Gregory of Nazianzus used it in relation to the union between the divinity and the humanity in Christ (cf. *Ep.* 101 and *Or.* 38:13). While the notion was present within trinitarian theology prior to the use of the term, *perichoresis* itself was first employed on the trinitarian level by Pseudo-Cyril followed by John Damascene (see Prestige, *God in Patristic Thought*, pp. 282–301; Congar, *I Believe in the Holy Spirit*, Vol. III, pp. 36–43; and de Margerie, *The Christian Trinity in History*, pp. 178–86).

Concerning the Greek use of *perichoresis* and the Latin equivalents Boff writes:

> The Greek word has a double meaning, which explains why two words were used to translate it into Latin. Its first meaning is that of one thing being contained in another, dwelling in, being in another – a situation of fact, a static state. This understanding was translated by *circuminsessio*, a word derived from *sedere* and *sessio*, being seated, having its seat in, seat. Applied to the mystery of the communion of the Trinity this signified: one Person is in the others, surrounds the others on all sides (*circum-*), occupies the same space as the others, fills them with its presence. Its second meaning is active and signifies the interpenetration or interweaving of one Person with the others and in the others. This understanding seeks to express the living and eternal process of relating intrinsic to the three Persons, so that each is always penetrating the others. This meaning was translated as *circumincessio*, derived from *incedere*, meaning to permeate, compenetrate and interpenetrate (*Trinity and Society*, pp. 135–6).

become who they are, and they do so precisely in reciprocally interacting upon one another, simultaneously fashioning one another to be who they are and so becoming who they are in themselves. None of the persons is purely passive; not even the Holy Spirit.

In the present conception of the Trinity, unlike past conceptions, it is the role of the Spirit which makes this mutual co-inherence of action possible and intelligible. The Father begets the Son in the spiration of the Spirit and so it is the Spirit that makes the Father to be the Father of the Son and makes the Son to be the Son of the Father. The Spirit proceeds from the Father and the Son and does so by conforming each to be in relation to the other, and so becomes distinct in himself in his mutual relation to them as the love by which they come to be who they are for one another.

This *perichoresis* of *action* on the part of all three persons completely revolutionizes the *perichoresis* of the East and the circumincession of the West. For the East, the *perichoresis* of the divine persons was founded primarily on the Father as the sole source of the divinity of the Son and the Holy Spirit. While the Orthodox perception of the *perichoresis* was more dynamic than that of the Latins, yet precisely because it was founded upon the Father, it could not truly account for why the persons mutually co-inhere since the Son and the Spirit proceed 'out from' the Father in a linear fashion modeled after Neo-Platonic emanationism. Similarly, while the West maintained the circumincession by having the Father and Son reciprocally loving one another in the bond of the Spirit, the Spirit himself is merely passive. The dynamic nature of the *perichoresis* is lost. He is simply what the Father and the Son share with one another.[42]

While, both in the East and the West, the *perichoresis* or circumincession has been seen as *the result* of the begetting and the spirating, I have emphasized the *perichoresis* of the actions themselves. Because the Father spirates the Spirit as he begets the Son, for it is

---

[42] See Kasper, *The God of Jesus Christ*, pp. 283–4.

in the Spirit that the Son is begotten, there is a *perichoresis* of action – the acts of begetting and spiration co-inhere in one another and thus account for why the persons themselves co-inhere. Actually, the persons themselves are the co-inhering acts. This *perichoresis* of the trinitarian act gives an unprecedented dynamism to the persons and to their life within the Trinity.

Furthermore, the present conception of the Trinity has obtained a symmetry never before attained.[43] This newfound symmetry is due precisely to the fact that the Holy Spirit now plays an active role within the Trinity. The one act by which the one God is a trinity of persons is the Father begetting the Son in the Spirit, in which act both the Father and the Son are conformed to be Father and Son in the Spirit. This symmetry is clearly seen when we examine why the Holy Spirit is a subsistent relation, and thus a person, along with the Father and the Son.[44]

---

[43] Kasper comments that the West, unlike the East, has a more symmetrical representation of the Trinity since the Holy Spirit 'rounded off' the trinitarian actions in a 'circular movement'. The Spirit is the bond of love between the Father and the Son. Nonetheless, Kasper believes that the West was not completely successful because it equally wished to maintain that the Father was the source of both the Son and the Spirit (*The God of Jesus Christ*, p. 216).

I would argue that the real cause for the lack of symmetry within the conception of the Trinity, both in the East and the West, is primarily due to the inactivity of the Holy Spirit as he proceeds from the Father and the Son. They are active in their love for one another, but as their love for one another the Spirit is purely passive. Once the Holy Spirit comes forth from the Father as the one in whom the Son is begotten, so conforming the Father to be Father and the Son to be Son, a symmetry of action and thus a symmetry of *perichoresis* within the Trinity is secured.

[44] Boff argues for a view very similar to the one I have just expressed.

Using the descriptive terminology of tradition, we would say: the Father 'begets' the Son in the bosom of the Spirit (*Filius a Patre Spirituque*), or the Father 'breathes out' the Spirit together with the Son (*Spiritus a Patre Filioque*) ... In this way we should have a trinitarian equilibrium since all is triadic and perichoretically implied; all is shared, circulated,

Subsistent Relations:
Why is the Holy Spirit a Person?

Why Gregory of Nazianzus, Augustine, and Aquinas have stressed that the persons of the Trinity are differentiated only by their relations to one another now becomes evident, in a new way. For example, for Aquinas the Father, the Son, and the Holy Spirit are persons (distinct subjects) because they subsist, as who they are, only as they relate to one another. Only their relations specify and determine their unique ontological subjectivities. The Father subsists as Father only in relation to the Son and Holy Spirit. The Son subsists as Son only in

> reciprocally received, united through communion ...This perichoretic communion does not result from the Persons, but is simultaneous with them, originates with them. They are what they are because of their intrinsic, essential communion. If this is so, it follows that everything in God is triadic, everything is *Patreque, Filioque* and *Spirituque.* The coordinate conjunction 'and' applies absolutely to the three Persons: 'and' is always and everywhere ...The Son is 'begotten' by the Father in the Holy Spirit. Put figuratively: the Father 'begets' the Son virginally in the maternal-virginal womb of the Holy Spirit. In trinitarian terms, The Father 'begets' the Son *Spirituque,* that is, in communion with the Holy Spirit (*Trinity and Society*, pp. 6, 146–7; see also pp. 84, 204–5, 236).

Boff, through his use of the phrases *Patreque, Filioque, Spirituque,* is striving to articulate that each person of the Trinity is constituted in a simultaneous and an active subsistent relationship with one another. While I endorse his understanding of *Filioque* and *Spirituque,* I find his use of *Patreque* ambiguous. The Father does not come forth from the Son and the Holy Spirit similar as to the way the Son and the Spirit come forth from him. However, if he is attempting to say what I have stated above, that is, that the Spirit conforms the Father to be the Father as the Father breathes forth the Spirit, and that the Son helps establish the Father as Father as he actively cries out 'Abba!' in his being begotten, then I could agree with his notion of *Patreque.*

This lack of clarity is also seen when Boff states that there is no 'causal' order of relationships within the Trinity; that is, the Father is in no sense first. All is one simultaneous act of inter-related being and communion (see ibid, pp. 146, 206). What Boff wants to avoid is a sequential priority and precedence among the persons of the Trinity, but in so doing he becomes vague on the need to maintain an order of origin and derivation founded upon the Father.

relation to the Father and the Holy Spirit. And the Holy Spirit subsists as Holy Spirit only in relation to the Father and the Son.[45] Aquinas emphasized that the Father, the Son, and the Holy Spirit subsist as relations of opposition; that is, it is their relations that distinguish them one from another.[46] This is true, but I would want to add that in the present conception of the Trinity, the persons subsist not only in opposition to one another, but also in complementarity to one another. They consummate one another. Because each of the persons now actively plays a role in determining the subjectivity of the others, they complement one another. The Father is Father not only in opposition to the Son and the Son is Son not only in opposition to the Father, but they also, in their relatedness, complement one another as being, respectively, Father for the Son

---

[45] Gregory of Nazianzus wrote that 'the difference of manifestation, if I may so express myself, or rather of their mutual relations one to another, has caused the difference of their names' (*Oratio*, 31, 9). See Augustine, *De Trinitate*, VI:6, 9, 11, 14; VII:9. Also Aquinas defines a divine person as 'a relation as subsisting' (*S.T.*, I, 29, 4; see also I, 40).

Kasper states: 'The three persons of the Trinity are pure relationality; they are relations in which the one nature of God exists in three distinct and non-interchangeable ways. They are subsistent relations' (*The God of Jesus Christ*, p. 309; see pp. 279–81, 289–90). See also W. Hill, *The Three-Personed God*, pp. 71–3; Boff, *Trinity and Society*, pp. 57, 92, 127, 138; and Pannenberg, *Systematic Theology*, Vol. 1, pp. 322–5, 428–31.

To say that the three persons of the Trinity are subsistent relations does not mean that their personhood is something distinct from the being of God, as if to be a subsistent relation is similar to the smile on the Cheshire cat – a smile with no being (catness) behind it. (This concern, along with the simile, was expressed to me by Fr Edward Yarnold.) To be a subsistent relation means tht the divine persons subsist or exist as God only in relation to each other. The being of God is the inter-relatedness of the subsistent persons. See Moltmann, *The Trinity and the Kingdom of God*, pp. 171–4.

LaCugna presents a brief summary of the Stoic and Aristotelian background to relations as well the notion of trinitarian relations in the Cappadocians, Augustine, and Aquinas (see *God For Us*, pp. 58–9, 60–6, 85–91, 152–7).

[46] See *S.T.*, I, 36, 2; I, 40, 2.

and Son for the Father. This complementarity of the persons as subsistent relations is due again to the Holy Spirit. By being the one in whom the Father begets the Son and so is Father for the Son, and by being the one in whom the Son is begotten and so is Son for the Father, the Holy Spirit subsists as the source of their complementarity.[47] The Trinity of persons then subsists in opposition to one another only as complementary relations.

Thus the distinction of persons and the unity of the persons are founded upon the fact that they are subsistent relations. What makes them three is the very same thing that makes them one – subsisting as pure relations. They only subsist as three distinct subjects in their oneness and they only exist as one in their specific threeness. The one nature of God and the trinity of persons are not then dialectically opposed. The one being or nature of God is the interrelationship of the three persons – opposition in complementarity. As subsistent relations the Father, the Son and Holy Spirit exist as one God.

Now what is new in the present conception of the Trinity is again the role of the Spirit as a subsistent relation. Within the tradition, we could more easily see that the terms 'Father' and 'Son' specify why they subsist only in relation to one another. But why does the Holy Spirit subsist as a distinct subject in relation to them? What is the content of this relationship? While the Holy Spirit is named Love and Gift (which are less than subjective or personal names), Aquinas states that the Holy Spirit really does not have a proper name, but can appropriately be called Holy Spirit because he is spirated and, like the Father and Son, he is both spirit and holy.[48] But why, if the Holy Spirit is a distinct subject, does he not have a

---

[47] Charles Massabki states that the Holy Spirit 'makes the Father and the Son exist only for each other' (*Who Is the Holy Spirit?* (New York: Alba House, 1979), p. 20).

[48] See *S.T.*, I, 27, 4, ad 3; I, 28, 4; I, 36, 1. Aquinas founded this understanding on St. Augustine. See *De Trinitate*, V:12.

proper name? What makes the Holy Spirit a person, a 'who'?

The Holy Spirit does not have a distinct name because he subsists precisely as the one in whom the Father and the Son are named. The Father subsists in relation to the Son (and so is named Father) *only in the Holy Spirit* by whom he begot the Son. The Son subsists in relation to the Father (and so is named Son) *only in the Spirit* who conformed him to be Son. The Spirit subsists as a pure relation together with the Father and the Son in that he sustains their relationship and so imparts or manifests their names. The Holy Spirit is the hidden or unnamed person or 'who' because the very nature of his subjectivity as a subsistent relation is to illuminate or, more deeply, to substantiate or person the Father and the Son for one another.[49] It could even be said that the Holy Spirit is the most personal of the trinitarian persons, and thus the most relational in his subjectivity, because he is the most translucent and transparent. Through him the Father and Son eternally gaze upon one another in love.[50]

---

[49] Gunton states: 'Not only must we say, with Augustine, that the Spirit is the unifying link between Father and Son; it is even more necessary to add that he is the focus of the distinctiveness of Father and Son – of their unique particularity …We may say that the Spirit's function in the Godhead is to particularize the hypostases' (*The One, The Three and The Many*, p. 190).

[50] Von Balthasar calls the Holy Spirit 'the ultimate Subject' (*Explorations in Theology III*, pp. 114–15).

The transparency of the Spirit's subjectivity further explains why God is defined as Spirit and Love in the Johannine writings. God is spirit not only in the sense that he is a spiritual being and he is love not only in the sense that he is all loving, but more precisely in the distinctively Christian sense that it is in the Holy Spirit that the Father and Son love one another. Durrwell states that 'the Spirit is God's unity in person' (*Holy Spirit of God*, p. 149; see also p. 150).

It is not surprising, then, that the Holy Spirit is often the 'forgotten' person of the Trinity. His very nature is to lie hidden and perform the humble task of revealing the Father and the Son to one another and to us. See Kasper, *The God of Jesus Christ*, pp. 198, 223.

This is in keeping with the Holy Spirit's economic mission. The role of the Spirit in the economy of salvation is not to make himself known, but to manifest the love of God the Father and Jesus as Son. Equally, the Spirit, by dwelling in us and transforming us into sons and daughters, inserts us into the life of the Trinity where the Father becomes our father and we, in turn, cry out with the Son, 'Abba!'

The traditions of both the East and the West have grappled with why the Holy Spirit is a person – a distinct subject or 'who'. This present understanding of the Holy Spirit as a subsistent relation and of the role he plays in relation to the Father and the Son not only upholds the Spirit's personhood, but also more thoroughly founds and defines it.

CHAPTER FIVE:

THE ECUMENICAL SIGNIFICANCE
OF THE THESIS

The controversy surrounding the *filioque* has divided the Orthodox
and Latin Churches for 1,200 years.[1] There have been numerous
attempts, both theological and conciliar, to mend the breach, none

---

[1] Congar presents an excellent brief history of the development of this
controversy (*I Believe in the Holy Spirit*, Vol. III, pp. 3–60). While the basis of the
controversy is found in the Pneumatology of the Cappadocians in the East and
Augustine in the West, the actual conflict did not arise until the time of Charlemagne
in the year 794 when a council was held in Frankfurt. This council condemned the
teachings of the Second Council of Nicea (787) on the veneration of images, and
proclaimed the *filioque*, defending its place in the Nicene-Constantinopolitan creed.
The *filioque*, first professed in Spain at the Third Council of Toledo in 589, was
subsequently inserted into the Creed in the last decade of the sixth century in Spain
and Gaul where the creed was recited at Mass. It came to Charlemagne via Alcuin
who had been familiar with it in England. At this time the *filioque* was thought to
be part of the original creed of Nicea-Constantinople. Despite pressure from
Charlemagne, Pope Leo III, while affirming its theological validity, refused to insert
it into the creed. The creed, containing the *filioque* clause, only came to be recited
in Rome in 1014 at the insistence of Emperor Henry II.

See also Heron, '"Who proceedeth from the Father and the Son": The Problem
of the Filioque', *Scottish Journal of Theology* 24 (1971) 149–66; Meyendorff, *Byzantine
Theology*, pp. 91–102; Moltmann, *The Trinity and the Kingdom of God*, pp. 178–80;
and D. Ritschl, 'The History of the Filioque Controversy', *Concilium: Conflicts about
the Holy Spirit* 128 (8/1979) 3–14.

of which has been fully satisfactory or successful.[2]

---

[2]   Emperor Michael VIII Palaeologus welcomed Pope Gregory X's call for a council of reunion. He hoped that union with Rome would protect his recently regained Empire from the new threat of King Charles of Anjou. Thus the Second Council of Lyons in 1274 declared that the Spirit proceeds 'eternally from Father and Son, not as from two sources (*principiis*) but as from a single source, not as a result of two spirations but rather of one spiration' (*Denz.-Schön*. 850). The union achieved between the Orthodox and the Latins proved unpopular in the East and ended in 1289 not long after Emperor Michael died.

A second attempt at reunion was made at the Council of Ferrara-Florence in 1438–9. It was argued that, while the East and the West held different views on the nature of the Spirit's procession, yet, because these views were held by holy and saintly men of both traditions in the past, neither could be wrong. Thus to say that the Spirit proceeds from the Father through the Son and to say that the Spirit proceeds from the Father and the Son must ultimately mean the same thing or at least be compatible. The Council therefore declared:

> that the Holy Spirit has his being eternally from the Father and the Son, that he has his essence and his subsistence both from the Father and from the Son together, and that he proceeds eternally from both as from a single principle and by a single spiration. We declare that what the holy doctors and Fathers say, that is, that the Holy Spirit proceeds from the Father through the Son, is intended to mean that the Son is also, according to the Greeks, the cause and, according to the Latins, the principle of the subsistence of the Holy Spirit, as the Father is. And since everything that belongs to the Father, the Father gives to his only begotten Son by begetting him, apart from being Father, the Son has it eternally from the Father, by whom he is eternally begotten, that the Holy Spirit proceeds from him. We define, moreover, that the explanation (or explicitation) of those words *Filioque* has been lawfully and reasonably added to the creed in order to declare the truth and because of the urgent need (*Denz.-Schön.*, 1300–2; trans. from Congar, *I Believe in the Holy Spirit*, Vol. III, p. 186).

The East, especially among the monks and the people of Constantinople with the urging of Mark Eugenicus, soon found the solution intolerable. With the fall of Constantinople in 1453 the union ended. Ritschl laments that 'the real theological dispute had become deplorably reduced to the bickerings and wranglings of ecclesiastical politics, and in these terms no solution was possible. Political intrigue, confused struggling for power and genuine theological learning had become

In this chapter I will examine the ecumenical significance of my proposed thesis; that is, that the Father begets the Son in the Spirit and thus that the Spirit proceeds from the Father as the one in whom the Son is begotten and so in turn proceeds from the Son as the one in whom and through whom the Son loves the Father. Does this trinitarian view liberate us from the *filioque* controversy? However, before I directly take up this question I would like briefly to examine some recent ecumenical developments in relation to the *filioque* controversy which would provide a context in which my thesis might find a welcome home.[3]

An Ecumenical Convergence

Firstly, the work of the Russian Church historian and theologian Boris Bolotov has provided an ecumenical framework in which the

---

too tangled up with each other ...' ('The History of the Filioque Controversy', p. 8). Nonetheless, as Congar states, the Council of Florence did become 'the basis of later unions, such as that achieved at Brest in 1596' (*I Believe in the Holy Spirit*, Vol. III, p. 186).

Moreover, Congar states:

> The indefeasible deposit of Florence is twofold: (1) the intention to recognize that the two formulae ['from the Father through the Son,' and 'from the Father and the Son'] were compatible and even equivalent – I would willingly say, that they were complementary; (2) the principle on the basis of which this intention was pursued, namely that the Fathers of the Church, inspired by the Holy Spirit, held, in communion, both formulae. Any new attempt to approach this question should take this as a point of departure and as a basis for discussion (ibid., p. 188; see also pp. 184–91).

See also de Margerie, *The Christian Trinity in History*, pp. 160–8.

[3] In the course of this study we have already seen points of convergence between my thesis and the work of other theologians, most notably, Boff, Durrwell, Moltmann, and Yarnold; but also Coffey, Clément, von Balthasar, and Pannenberg. Here I will look at some theological works and ecumenical dialogues which bear directly upon the issue of the *filioque*.

concerns of both the East and the West can seriously be considered.[4] While Bolotov wished to maintain that the Holy Spirit proceeds solely from the Father, he realized that the procession cannot be isolated from the generation of the Son, for the Spirit proceeds from the Father who is Father precisely because he begets the Son. It is the Father *of the Son* from whom the Spirit proceeds, and thus the procession of the Holy Spirit presupposes the begetting of the Son, otherwise it would not be from *the Father* that the Spirit proceeds. Thus he writes: 'I believe in the Holy Spirit who goes forth from the one only Father insofar as he begets the only Son' *(ek monou tou Patros, hos ton Monogene gennontos, ekporeuomenon).*[5] Bolotov clearly grasped that while the Spirit proceeds from the Father, the Spirit's procession is intimately linked with the generation of the Son. The Holy Spirit proceeds from the Father only in so far as the Father is the Father of the Son.

I believe that my thesis is not only in sympathy with Bolotov's ecumenical endeavor, but that it is also particularly compatible with it. It can hopefully help specify why it is that the Spirit proceeds from the Father as the Father of the Son; namely, because the Holy Spirit goes forth from the Father as the one in whom the Father begets the Son. Thus the Spirit proceeds from the Father of the Son

---

[4]   Boris Bolotov (1853–1900) wrote an anonymous article ('By a Russian Theologian') entitled: 'Thesen über das *Filioque*', *Revue Internationale de Théologie*, 24 (1898) 271–89.

Bolotov proposed that there are three levels of doctrinal statements. The first is the actual dogmas promulgated at ecumenical councils and professed in the creeds. The second is that of individual theologies, and the third is that of theologoumena, that is, expressions of the faith held by the Fathers of both the East and the West prior to the Schism and accepted by the undivided Church. In light of this, he proposed 27 theses concerning the issue of the *filioque*.

For a list of some of the more important theses see Congar, *I Believe in the Holy Spirit*, Vol. III, pp. 194–5.

[5]   As quoted by J.-M. Garrigues, 'A Roman Catholic View of the Position Now Reached in the Question of the Filioque', *Spirit of God, Spirit of Christ*, p. 153.

because it is in the Spirit that the Father, by begetting the Son in the Spirit, also constitutes himself as the Father of the Son. The procession of the Spirit, then, does not just presuppose the begetting of the Son, but is also simultaneous with and constitutive of the begetting of the Son.[6]

---

[6]   Bolotov's work has influenced a number of contemporary theologians and thus the present thesis would also intersect with their own understanding of the procession of the Holy Spirit.

Moltmann, for example, in commenting on Bolotov, states:

> If then God as Father breathes forth the Holy Spirit, the Spirit proceeds *from the Father of the Son*. His procession therefore presupposes (1) the generation of the Son, (2) the existence of the Son, and (3) the mutual relation of the Father and the Son. The Son is the logical presupposition and the material precondition for the procession of the Spirit from the Father, but he is not an additional accompanying source for him. The procession of the Spirit from the Father must be substantially distinguished from the generation of the Son by the Father, and yet related to it ('Theological Proposals Towards the Resolution of the Filioque Controversy', *Spirit of God, Spirit of Christ*, p. 168; see also pp. 164–73).

While I agree with Moltmann's primary concerns, I would make two qualifications. Firstly the Son is a derivative source of the Holy Spirit in that, having been begotten by the Father in the Spirit, the Son loves the Father in the same Spirit, for it is in the Spirit that he is constituted as Son. Secondly, I would want to make the same qualification with regard to Moltmann as I made in relation to Bolotov. If the Father begets the Son in the Spirit then the sequentialism is done away with. The Father does not first beget the Son so that the Son then becomes the precondition for the procession of the Spirit. Rather the begetting of the Son is the precondition of the proceeding of the Spirit in the sense that the Father only begets the Son in or by the Spirit. The Spirit proceeds from the Father as the one in whom the Son is begotten.

I believe Moltmann would agree with my concern, for he states elsewhere that 'the two "processions" are simultaneous and in common' (*The Trinity and the Kingdom of God*, p. 184; see also pp. 182–7).

For other examples of theologians who find significance in or are influenced by Bolotov see Garrigues, *Spirit of God, Spirit of Christ*, pp. 149–63; D. Staniloae, 'The Procession of the Holy Spirit from the Father and His Relation to the Son, as the Basis of our Deification and Adoption', *Spirit of God, Spirit of Christ*, pp. 174–86; Boff, *The Trinity and Society*, pp. 204–6; Congar, *I Believe in the Holy Spirit*, Vol.

Secondly, there has been some recent theological enthusiasm for, and ecumenical approval of, the expressions: 'The Spirit proceeds from the Father and abides in/rests upon/is received by the Son.' Pannenberg, for example, states that 'we can say only that the Spirit proceeds from the Father and is received by the Son'.[7] Boris Bobrinskoy similarly argues, in a manner comparable to my own arguments, that since the earthly life of Jesus demonstrates that he is the supreme bearer of the Holy Spirit, this 'theological vision attains to the intuition of the eternal mystery of the Holy Spirit, no longer as proceeding from the Son, or through the Son, but as resting on the Son from all eternity'.[8] Clément also argues that the name 'Christ' implies not only an earthly but also an eternal anointing. 'Now the Father is the one who from all eternity "anoints" the Son by causing the Spirit to rest on him, or rather in him, as an unction, the "oil of gladness" of the psalm, because the Spirit is the joy of the divine communion.'[9] Moltmann sees the Spirit eternally resting in the Son.[10] Moreover, the agreed statement between the Orthodox and Reformed Churches states that 'the Son is eternally begotten of the Father and the Spirit eternally proceeds from the Father and abides in the Son.'[11]

III, pp. 192–8; S. Virgulin, 'Il Filioque Nel Pensiero Del Teologo Russo V.B. Bolotov', *Credo In Spiritum Sanctum*, Vol. 1, pp. 355–63.

[7]   *Systematic Theology*, Vol. 1, p. 317; cf. p. 358.

[8]   'The Filioque Yesterday and Today', *Spirit of God, Spirit of Christ*, p. 144.

[9]   *The Roots of Christian Mysticism*, pp. 58–9.

[10]   See Moltmann, *The Spirit of Life*, p. 307.

[11]   'Agreed Statement on the Holy Trinity', *Theological Dialogue Between Orthodox and Reformed Churches*, Vol. 2, p. 222. See also the working paper in the same volume (p. 111) and the Introduction, p. xv. Most of this documentation can also be found in *Trinitarian Perspectives*.

What is said here is again quite close to the present proposal. What my thesis adds is the rationale for this abiding, resting, or receiving. The reason that the Spirit proceeds from the Father and so 'abides in', 'rests upon', or 'is received by' the Son is that the Father begets the Son in the Spirit, and so the Spirit abides in or rests upon or is received by the Son as the one in whom or by whom he is begotten of the Father. The abiding, resting, and receiving is not subsequent to the begetting, but is constitutive of the begetting.[12]

The Anglican-Orthodox agreed statements are less theologically sophisticated than those between the Orthodox and the Reformed Churches and do not use any of the above expressions. See *Anglican-Orthodox Dialogue: The Moscow Statement 1976* nn. 19–21 and *Anglican-Orthodox Dialogue: The Dublin Statement 1984*, nn. 44–6. Both are published together, K. Ware and C. Davey (eds) (London: SPCK, 1985).

For a brief historical study of the various ecumenical dialogues, see Congar, *I Believe in the Holy Spirit*, Vol. III, pp. 192–8.

[12] Staniloae finds such idioms as 'abiding in' or 'resting upon' to be historically and theologically founded upon the work of St. John Damascene and St. Gregory Palamas. 'For this reason, Christ is called the Treasurer of the Spirit' ('The Procession of the Holy Spirit from the Father, *Spirit of God, Spirit of Christ*, p. 181).

The expression 'the Spirit proceeds from the Father and receives from the Son' is sometimes used. See, for example, Moltmann, 'Theological Proposals', *Spirit of God, Spirit of Christ*, p. 169, and his *The Trinity and the Kingdom of God*, pp. 185–7, and also in the 'Agreed Statement on the Trinity', *Theological Dialogue Between Orthodox and Reformed Churches*, Vol. 2, p. 224.

I find this idiom, which goes back to Epiphanius, ambiguous, particularly the word 'from'. Since it is often used as an ecumenical alternative to the *filioque*, it would not seem to imply that the Spirit is in some sense constituted as a person by the Son. However, this is precisely how Moltmann interprets it. Though the Holy Spirit proceeds solely from the Father and so is constituted in his divinity, yet he receives from the Father and from the Son his distinct subjectivity. To the question, What does the Holy Spirit receive from the Son?, Moltmann replies:

Our proposed answer would be: the Holy Spirit has from the Father his perfect, divine existence (*hypostasis, hyparxis*) and receives from the Son his relational form (*eidos, prosopon*). Although the procession of the Holy Spirit's divine existence must emphatically be ascribed to the Father *alone*, yet it must be equally firmly recognized that its form or visage is

In the context of these ecumenical developments, which are closely and positively related to what I am proposing, I will now offer my thesis as an integral (if small) component for a comprehensive and satisfactory resolution to the *filioque* impasse. I hope that my thesis helps transcend the controversy by placing the procession of the Holy Spirit in an entirely new context. There are four reasons for this hope.

Freed From Foreign Philosophies

The cause of this impasse, as I have already argued, is that neither the East's nor the West's conception of the Trinity is sufficiently biblical, and that they are scripturally inadequate precisely because both contain foreign and non-biblical philosophical presuppositions. Orthodox trinitarian theology, biblical though it is, has been fashioned in the mold of Neo-Platonic emanationism producing a linear sequential conception of the Trinity. This residue of Neo-Platonic sequentialism, while less evident in Western trinitarian thought, nonetheless remains and is reinforced by Aristotelian epistemology.

As I have contended throughout, the present conception of the Trinity is purged of the remnants of Neo-Platonic emanationism and transcends Aquinas' use of Aristotle, and so offers a solution, hopefully, acceptable to both sides of the debate. This liberation was won by conceiving the immanent Trinity within an ontology that is itself inherent within the economic trinitarian witness of the New Testament. It newly locates the procession of the Holy Spirit in a way that, as we will now explain, escapes the *filioque* polemic.

Safeguarding and Transcending the Concerns

The conception of the Trinity presented here not only safeguards the interests of each party, but actually clarifies and deepens their

---

moulded by the Father and by the Son. This is why he is also called 'the Spirit of the Son' (*The Trinity and the Kingdom of God*, p. 186).

distinctive, authentic concerns. The East rightly demands that any true understanding of the Trinity must not only preserve but actually advocate the monarchy of the Father as the principal source of the Son and the Holy Spirit. The East believes this is essential for assuring the distinct personality of the Holy Spirit, for the Spirit is the Spirit precisely because he proceeds from the Father. Despite the disclaimers of the West, the Orthodox assert that the Latins jeopardize both the Father's monarchy and the Spirit's distinct personality in the *filioque*, firstly by compromising the monarchy of the Father in that the Spirit also proceeds from the Son, secondly by confusing the persons in that the Son now becomes a 'second Father' in the procession of the Spirit, and thirdly by diminishing the distinctiveness of the Holy Spirit as proceeding from the Father alone.[13]

The proposition set forth here that the Father begets the Son in the Spirit confirms and stresses that the Spirit principally proceeds from the Father. The Spirit must proceed from the one source of the Father because it is only in the procession of the Spirit that the Father begets the Son. Not only, then, is the monarchy of the Father brought into relief, but equally the distinct procession of the Spirit from him. The Spirit's specific personality is also clearly depicted since an unconfused distinction is made between the procession of the Spirit and the generation of the Son. The Spirit proceeds as the one in whom the Son is begotten. The Orthodox should not only find this conception of the Trinity reassuring, but actually helpful in sustaining their authentic objectives.

The West has argued that, while the Spirit proceeds principally from the Father, he derivatively proceeds from the Son as well. In so

---

[13] For expressions or summaries of these types of arguments among Orthodox theologians see: 'Memorandum', *Spirit of God, Spirit of Christ*, pp. 12, 14, 17, 22; also in the same volume see M. Orphanos, 'The Procession of the Holy Spirit according to Certain Later Greek Fathers', pp. 43, 47; and D. Ritschl, 'Historical Development and Implications of the *Filioque* Controversy', p. 59. Also C. Voulgaris, 'The Biblical and Patristic Doctrine of the Trinity', *Theological Dialogue Between Orthodox and Reformed Churches*, Vol. 2, p. 126.

arguing, the West contends that this better assures the divinity of the Holy Spirit, the unity of the Trinity, and the specificity of the procession in contrast to the generation. The West also maintains that this is in keeping with the New Testament, in that, while the Spirit is explicitly said to proceed from the Father, the economy of salvation demonstrates that the Spirit also proceeds from the Son.[14]

Again the conception of the Trinity presented here not only secures these concerns, but actually explains and enhances their validity (hopefully without offending the interests of the Orthodox). The fact that the Father spirates the Spirit in the begetting of the Son, not only allows the West to hold firmly, along with the East, the monarchy of the Father, but also shows why the Spirit proceeds also from the Son. The Son, being begotten by the Father, is conformed as Son by the Spirit (of sonship) and so the Spirit proceeds from him as the identical Love for the Father in whom he himself is begotten.[15]

Such a view highlights the equal divinity of the persons and their interrelated unity. At the same time the singularity of the procession is defined and assigned specific content, something that both the East and the West have been endeavoring to articulate and

---

[14]   For arguments and summaries favoring the Western view of the *filioque* see Boff, *Trinity and Society*, p. 83; Ritschl, 'Historical Development and Implications of the *Filioque* Controversy', *Spirit of God, Spirit of Christ*, p. 62; Sherry, *Spirit and Beauty*, p. 94.

[15]   Durrwell is correct when he states:

If the Spirit is possessed in common, in an identical fullness, *he is nevertheless possessed differently*. For the Father begets in the Spirit, whereas the Son is begotten in the Spirit. The Father is the source flowing into the Son; all is given by the Father and all is possessed in common; nothing distinguishes the Son, except that he is the Son and not the Father, and that *he possesses the Spirit by receiving him*. The treasure is possessed in common, but with the difference that distinguishes the Father and the Son (*Holy Spirit of God*, p. 142; see also pp. 140–5).

establish since the fourth century.

However, I also believe that what I have proposed here not only reinforces the authentic interests and reconciles the divergent concerns of the East and the West, but also transcends the continuing controversy. Only if my proposal transcends the *filioque* deadlock will the East and West be able to use it to free themselves from their present theological and doctrinal impasse.[16] By giving the Holy Spirit his proper role within the Trinity the controversy over the procession is surmounted for the entire conception of the Trinity is now transfigured and redesigned. Not only does the Holy Spirit proceed principally from the Father (the concern of the East) and derivatively from the Son (the concern of the West), but the Spirit in proceeding from the Father as the one in whom the Son is begotten now actively conforms the Father to be Father for the Son and conforms the Son to be Son for the Father. It is this active role of the Spirit, by which he himself is defined in relation to the Father and the Son, which neither the East nor the West has appreciated. Yet it is precisely this

---

[16] In a desire to find common ecumenical ground and a unity of faith, it is sometimes proposed that both the East and the West should mutually accept the expression that the Holy Spirit proceeds from the Father 'through the Son'. This idiom has an ancient tradition in both the East and the West, and, above all, it avoids the historical and theological morass of the *filioque*.

I am skeptical about such a proposal. It is ambiguous as to exactly what 'through the Son' means. How and why does the Spirit proceed from the Father through the Son and how does this procession through the Son affect the Holy Spirit? These questions have never been fully addressed. 'Through the Son' was primarily used in the first instance to express the economic Trinity, that is, that the Spirit proceeds from the Father and is given to us through the Son. As such, how the expression applies to the immanent Trinity has never been fully articulated and when it has been applied to the immanent Trinity something like the *filioque* springs up. The Spirit proceeds from the Father through the Son and back again to the Father.

For East and West to fall back on the expression 'through the Son' is not to solve the problem of the *filioque*, but to avoid it. Too much history has been lived and too much theology has been developed to dodge the issue. For a true ecumenical solution to be found, the *filioque* must be directly confronted and surmounted.

active role of the Spirit which safeguards their concerns and even transcends them.

Because the Holy Spirit is given his rightful place within the Trinity, performing the singular role that is appropriate to him, the Trinity acquires, as I noted earlier, a more symmetrical and harmonious form. Not only do the Father and Son actively constitute the Trinitarian life, but also the Holy Spirit. It is this activity of the Holy Spirit that actually assures and constitutes the symmetry and the unity of the persons. The one eternal act by which the Trinity is the Trinity – the Father begetting the Son in the Spirit and the Son loving the Father in the same Spirit – is performed now by each of the specific persons in their own singular manner. This is something neither the East or the West has been able to establish, but I offer my thesis as a possible solution to the theological division between them.

Correcting Ecclesiological Distortions

According to some Orthodox theologians, the *filioque* has subverted and deformed an authentic understanding of the Church. They have argued that all the exaggerations (evils) of the Latin Church find their source in the *filioque*. Because the *filioque* subordinates the Spirit to the Son, the West has fallen in Christomonism. This in turn has subordinated the gifts and life of the Spirit to the law and the institution. Freedom in the Spirit has given way to legalism and power. The prophetic and the conciliar have been subdued by the magisterium and the Petrine primacy. The rational has replaced the mystical. The laity have become subservient to the clergy.[17]

---

[17]   The most recent and ardent exponent of this view has been V. Lossky. See his *The Mystical Theology of the Eastern Church*, especially pp. 156–95, and 'The Procession of the Holy Spirit in the Orthodox Triadology', *Eastern Churches Quarterly* 7 (1948) 31–52. Clément has expressed some of these same concerns, though in a more recent work he has been more conciliatory. See *L'Église Orthodoxe* (Paris: 1961), p. 50, and *The Roots of Christian Mysticism*, pp. 70–2.

There may be some truth to these charges, but here is not the place to sort out and nuance their validity. Here I would briefly argue that, hopefully, my thesis provides new balance to the roles of the Son and the Spirit within ecclesiology.

Because within my trinitarian reconception both the Son and the Spirit play active and symmetrical roles within the Trinity, this would in turn balance out the functions they perform within the economy of salvation, particularly within the life of the Church. Since the Father begets the Son in and by the Spirit, the Spirit can no longer be seen as inferior to him. Thus the Spirit's life and vitality within the Church is once more founded upon the vital role he plays within the trinitarian life. Neither the Son nor the body of Christ – the Church – can possess life without the Spirit. Equally, since the Son loves the Father in the same Spirit in whom he is begotten, the Spirit is also the Spirit of the Son. Thus, within the life of the Church the Spirit always furthers the glory of Jesus and nourishes the life and helps establish the right order of his body.[18]

For surveys of and comments upon the issues Lossky raised see: A. de Halleux, 'Orthodoxie et Catholicisme: du personnalisme en pneumatologie', *Revue Théologique de Louvain*, 6 (1975) 13–14; 'Introduction', *Spirit of God, Spirit of Christ*, pp. 16–18; Congar, *I Believe in the Holy Spirit*, Vol. III, pp. 208–12; Kasper, *Jesus The Christ*, pp. 256–9; and Moltman, *History and the Triune God*, pp. 58–9.

Not all Orthodox theologians would support Lossky's view. See, for example, Evdokimov, *L'Esprit-Saint dans la Tradition Orthodoxe*, and S. Bulgakov, *Le Paraclet* (Paris: Aubier 1946), pp. 124, 141). See also de Halleux, 'Towards an Ecumenical Agreement on the Procession of the Holy Spirit and the Addition of the Filioque to the Creed', *Spirit of God, Spirit of Christ*, pp. 71–4.

[18] Clément similarly writes in relation to this issue:

Thus the relationship of the Son and the Spirit is seen to be one of mutual service. The Spirit comes from the Father in the Son and manifests him. The Son is born of the Father in the Spirit and is manifested by the Spirit. And both reveal the Father. In the Church the same reciprocity and the same mutual service must exist between the priesthood, which bears witness to the sacramental presence of Christ, and prophecy, which reveals the freedom of each conscience in the Holy Spirit (*The Roots of Christian Mysticism*, p. 70).

Faithfully Enhancing the Tradition

Both the Orthodox and the Latins may now ask: 'Is this new trinitarian proposal in conformity with the councils and the creeds?' Clearly, no council or creed has proclaimed what I have proposed. Yet despite the absence of my trinitarian proposal within the consiliar traditions of both the East and the West, it denies nothing that the councils have defined or the creeds proclaimed.[19] Moreover, I maintain that not only is it in conformity with what has been defined and professed, but it also, as the above hopefully demonstrates, actually advances the doctrinal understanding of the Trinity. It is expressly because it advances this authentic doctrinal understanding in an orthodox manner that the *filioque* debate is transcended and surmounted.[20]

It would be appropriate to mention here that the present understanding of the Trinity also facilitates Catholic-Protestant rapprochement. The Protestant Reformers accused the Catholic Church of legalism with a hierarchical emphasis, and so leaving no room for the prophetic. By allowing the Holy Spirit his proper place within the Trinity, this helps redress the concerns of Protestant theology.

[19] Yarnold maintains that such a proposal is in keeping with the demands of the Athanasian Creed. See Yarnold, 'The Trinitarian Implications of Luke and Acts', p. 32.

[20] I desire that Orthodox and Latin theologians thoroughly scrutinize my proposal, not only to determine its orthodoxy, but hopefully also as a catalyst to further the unity between the Churches. I am sure that I have said things that each side might find debatable, but I hope I have said enough to which each can agree so as to help is some small way to stimulate some common accord.

CHAPTER SIX:

LIVING THE LIFE OF THE TRINITY

This concluding chapter will briefly examine some of the pastoral and spiritual implications of the trinitarian theology advanced here. What is said about grace, the Church, and the sacraments will only be cursory. A full study goes beyond the scope of this work and would demand more expertise in ecclesiology and liturgy than I possess. My hope, though, is that the present trinitarian conception will foster a refreshing and realistic sense of the relevance of the Trinity for the Christian life. Only as a theology of the Trinity nurtures the lives of Christians will it actually carry out the task required – that of cultivating faith, intensifying hope, and fathering love.

The Economic and the Immanent Trinity

The major pastoral and spiritual benefit of the present trinitarian proposal is the close alignment between the economic Trinity and the immanent Trinity – indeed, their real identification. By thoroughly patterning the relationships between the Father, the Son, and the Holy Spirit within the immanent Trinity upon their economic missions as portrayed in the New Testament, we can recognize, in an unprecedented manner, that these missions, by which the immanent Trinity is revealed, make possible our entrance into

the immanent trinitarian life as the trinity of persons themselves
live it. The revelation of the immanent Trinity within the divine
economy is therefore inherently soteriological. Thus there is an
intrinsic and indispensable bond between the revelation of the Trinity
and our life within it.[1]
For example, the Father revealed himself as Father in the
sending of the Son into the world and by incarnating him through
the power of the Holy Spirit, and similarly he manifested his
fatherhood through the raising of Jesus from the dead, making him
Lord by the power of the Holy Spirit. But in so doing he not only
revealed that he is the Father in himself, but also and concurrently
performed his fatherly task by which those who believe might possess
him as Father through the same Holy Spirit. Again, the Son, in
becoming man and by dying on the cross, not only revealed that he
truly is the Son, but he also fulfilled his filial responsibility by which
those who believe in him receive his Spirit of sonship, and so become
his brothers and sisters in union with the Father. Or again, the Holy
Spirit, by coming to dwell in those who believe, not only revealed
himself, but in so doing transformed believers into the likeness of
the Son so as to have God as their Father. The present trinitarian
theology confirms that the actions of the persons of the Trinity in
the economy of salvation, by which they reveal who they are in
themselves and as they relate to one another, are the very same actions
by which they make possible our incorporation into the life of the
immanent Trinity.

It must be reiterated, though, that such an inherent link

---

[1] Kasper writes that the major challenge facing theologians is that of making
the Trinity relevant to our daily lives:

> They will not succeed in once again making the trinitarian confession a
> vital part of experiential faith unless they are able to bring home to
> Christians the importance of this confession for their salvation. This in
> turn means that they must pay greater attention to the connection between
> the economic Trinity and the immanent Trinity (*The God of Jesus Christ*,
> p. 263).

between the economic and the immanent Trinity and our incorporation into the Trinity has been established only because this study has re-envisioned the Trinity. The tether which binds this whole theology together is that as the Father begets the Son in the Spirit so too are we adopted as children of the Father in the Spirit. To deny the proper role of the Spirit within the Trinity is to conceptually sever the economic from the immanent Trinity, thereby implicitly cleaving our relationship to the trinity of persons as they are in themselves.[2]

The Trinity and Grace

Within this study the economic Trinity has become a mirror in which we gaze upon the immanent Trinity. Moreover, having peered into the inner life of the Trinity through the mirror of the economic Trinity, we can now see with greater depth the life Christians live within the Trinity.

The theology of grace then acquires a fresh spiritual realism and practicality. The ontology of grace is analogous to the ontology of the Trinity and inseparably connected with it. Upon conversion, through faith and baptism, the Holy Spirit comes to dwell in us and transforms or conforms us into adopted sons and daughters of the Father. Thus grace is first and foremost the uncreated life and presence of the Holy Spirit by which we share in the very life of the Trinity itself. We actually relate to the Father in an analogous manner to that of the Son, and we do so precisely because, like the Son, the Holy Spirit has conformed us into sons. The Spirit dwelling in us is the Spirit of sonship by which the Father conforms and begets us in the likeness of his eternal Son and so truly becomes our Father. The created effect in us, sanctifying or habitual grace, secured through the indwelling of the Spirit, is that we are actually related to the Father and Son as they are to one another. We now subjectively

---

[2] See Excursus Two for a response to LaCugna's view that the distinction between the immanent and economic Trinity must be abandoned.

subsist as Christians in relation to the Father and the Son, and we do so because, like them, we share in the common Love and Life of the Spirit by which they themselves subsist. This imparts new vividness to the biblical truth that we literally share in God's divine nature (see 2 Pet. 1:4).[3]

Baptism in the Spirit

The contemporary experience of Baptism in the Spirit as witnessed within the Pentecostal or Charismatic Renewal is strengthened and authenticated by this trinitarian theology.[4] Baptism in the Spirit is nothing more, and nothing less, than the experience of this life within

---

[3]   The East has traditionally stressed the divinizing effects of grace. Irenaeus held that we have taken on incorruptibility and immortality only because the Son of God has assumed our corruptibility and mortality (see *Adv. Haer.*, III, 19, 1). Athanasius articulated the foundational principle of all later Eastern theology of grace: 'He (the Son) became man (*enanthrōpoiēsis*) that we might be made God (*theopoiēsis*)' (*De Incarnatione*, 54). See Basil the Great, *De Spir.*, 27, 68; *Ep.*, 8.5; Gregory of Nazianzus, *Or.*, 1, 5; 29, 19; 30, 21; 31, 28–9, and 45, 9; Gregory of Nyssa, *Antirrheticus Adversus Apollinarem*; and *Or. Catech.*, 33; and Cyril of Alexandria, *Joh.* 1, 9.

While the West, following Augustine, has emphasized the healing and medicinal purpose of grace, the divinizing effect of grace has not been entirely absent. See Augustine, *De Trinitate*, XIII:12; *Epist.*, 140, 10; and for Aquinas see *S.T.*, I, 43, 3, ad 1; IIa, 65, 5; IIa, 112, 1.

My view of grace is in basic agreement with M. de la Taille – see *The Hypostatic Union and Created Actuation by Uncreated Act* (West Baden Springs, IN: West Baden College, 1952). See also Kasper, *The God of Jesus Christ*, pp. 226–7.

[4]   As I have already stated in the Preface, this study actually grew out of my experience of Baptism in the Spirit. It was in considering the effects of this experience that I came to see that I had a new and deeper awareness of God the Father and my own status as a son. Equally, I had an experiental awareness of Jesus as the eternal Son. Both were the effect of the Holy Spirit's work within me. I came to see, through subsequently studying the scriptures, that my experience was in accord with the New Testament and that my experience, in some small analogous manner, corresponded to the trinitarian life of the Father, the Son, and the Holy Spirit, that is, that the Father begets the Son in the Spirit so that through the Spirit the Father is Father for the Son and the Son is Son for the Father.

the Trinity. The Father and the Son experience one another in and through the Holy Spirit. The Spirit conforms them to be for one another, and so they experience their common life together in the Spirit.

Baptism in the Spirit is for us an analogous encounter, founded upon grace, but now brought to the level of perceptible experience. Through Baptism in the Spirit, we experience within our own spirit – that facility or power within us to apprehend God in a discernible and tangible manner – the love of God the Father and our fellowship with Jesus as Lord and Savior. The Holy Spirit confirms within us the Lordship of Jesus as the eternal Son of God. In and through our apprehending of Jesus as Lord and Savior, the Holy Spirit concomitantly manifests the love of the Father for us, and thus we existentially discover, in the Spirit, our true dignity and status as his sons and daughters.[5]

Baptism in the Spirit then becomes the experiential foundation for the Christian's living contact with the Trinity. The Christian, through prayer, scripture, and the sacraments, is empowered to receive revelation, that is, the Father directly speaking to and acting within the person through the Son in the Spirit. Even here on earth the Christian begins to experience, on a daily basis, the heavenly life of the Trinity.

Thus the experienced reality of Baptism in the Spirit, whether

---

[5]   From my extensive personal experience of the Charismatic Renewal I have found that individuals, regardless of age, denominational affiliation, theological education, or maturity of faith, have come, through the experience of Baptism in the Spirit, to a lively awareness of the Trinity. Where prior to Baptism in the Spirit 'Charismatic' Christians were, for the most part, 'practical monotheists', after Baptism in the Spirit they manifest an experiential awareness of the distinctive and individual relationships which they possess with each person of the Trinity. The report by the Doctrine Commission of the Church of England, *We Believe in the Holy Spirit*, p. 22 confirms this finding. In a personal conversation with Dr Sarah Coakley, who conducted much of the fieldwork research and interviews of Anglican charismatics for this report, she corroborated that her findings coincided with my own experience.

called by this name or not, should not be viewed as an optional extra or as unnecessary to the Christian life.[6] Through Baptism in the Spirit our life within the Trinity moves from the realm of theological doctrine to that of lived experience. Actually, without such an experiential encounter, the most thoroughly orthodox doctrine of the Trinity remains, for the most part, merely a dogma to which one gives intellectual assent, and not a life-giving spring from which one drinks of the reality.[7]

The Church and Sacraments

By patterning the work of the Spirit within the Trinity upon his work within the world, we are better able to see that the Spirit not only inserts individuals into the life of the Trinity as the Trinity is, but also that the Spirit elevates the whole Church, the body of Christ, into the life of the Trinity as it is. Every baptized person, Jew and Gentile, now has access 'in one Spirit to the Father' (Eph. 2:18). 'For by one Spirit we were all baptized into one body – Jews or Greeks, slaves or free – and all were made to drink of one Spirit' (1 Cor. 12:13). All are fellow citizens of God's household built upon the apostles and prophets with Christ as cornerstone. In Christ 'the whole structure is joined together and grows into a holy temple in the Lord; in whom you also are built into it for a dwelling place of God in the Spirit' (Eph. 2:19–22; see also 1 Pet. 2:5). Through the Spirit,

---

[6] It should be noted that almost all the saints have had some type of experience comparable to that of Baptism in the Spirit. This experience so changed their lives that they were compelled to live differently and so grow in holiness. The experience of the saints should not be seen as exceptional, but as the paradigm, and thus the norm, for all Christians.

[7] While Baptism in the Spirit goes beyond evangelical conversion, yet the key to experiencing Baptism in the Spirit is the simple and universal call to repentance and faith. The difficulty is that, while many adults are baptized and confirmed, they have never personally acknowledged their sinfulness, nor fully repented for their sin. Equally, many adult Christians have never come to a personally mature and whole-hearted commitment to Jesus in faith.

the Church enters into the heavenly life and worship with all the
saints and angels exulting in the Father and the Son as they eternally
exult in themselves.

The Church, being a living temple of God, offers prayer and
worship in accordance with the pattern of life we now share with
the Father, the Son, and the Holy Spirit. In the liturgy, Christians
worship and thank the Father through the Son in the Holy Spirit.
As the Son eternally glorifies the Father in the Spirit, so now do
Christians. 'Through him, with him, in him; in the unity of the
Holy Spirit; all glory and honor is yours, almighty Father, forever
and ever.' Equally, as the Father glorifies the Son in the Spirit, so
within the liturgy the Father pours out his love and mercy upon us
through Christ in the Spirit.

Thus, in the Eucharist, we see this descending (economic) and
ascending (immanent) trinitarian pattern. By the power of the Holy
Spirit (the *epiclesis*), the Father transforms the bread and wine into
the risen and glorified body and blood of his Son, and in our
communion with the risen Lord we are suffused with the Spirit so as
to give glory and honor to the Father. In the Eucharist, we have a
true actual foretaste of our heavenly life with the Father, through
the Son and in the Holy Spirit.

The ministries and gifts (*charismata*) given to the Church
examplify this same trinitarian pattern, and through them the Church
manifests and advances the gospel and also intensifies this trinitarian
life within the Church itself. 'There are varieties of gifts, but the
same Spirit; and there are varieties of service, but the same Lord;
and there are varieties of working, but the same God who inspires
them all in every one' (1 Cor. 12:4–6). Through the Holy Spirit the
Father animates all the ministries and gifts within the Church so
that the work of his Son may continue.

These ministries (apostles, preachers, teachers, prophets) and
gifts (wisdom, knowledge, miracles, healing, tongues), given by the
Spirit to the Church, allow the Church to experience on earth the
heavenly life, that is, our life with the Trinity (see 1 Cor. 12:7–11,

Rom. 12:6–8). Here on earth they manifest and build up our heavenly life with the Father in the Son, and they do so precisely because they are performed by the power of the Spirit.

God All in All

Lastly, our trinitarian proposal affords us a better vantage-point from which to perceive that the life lived with the Trinity here truly mirrors and advances the life we will live with the Trinity in heaven. The exact same relationships we have formed with the Father and the Son and the Holy Spirit here on earth will find their completion and fulfillment in heaven. There is no discrepancy between the two.

From all eternity, from before the foundation of the world, God the Father called and predestined us to be his people – holy, blameless, and full of love; that is, to be his adopted sons. He has accomplished this work through his Son in whom we have the forgiveness of our sins and in whom all things find their unity. Through faith we 'were sealed with the promised Holy Spirit, which is the guarantee of our inheritance until we acquire possession of it, to the praise of his glory' (Eph. 1:13–14). At the end of time, after all have found unity in Christ through the Spirit, 'the Son himself will also be subjected to him who put all things under him, that God may be all in all' (1 Cor. 15:28). Until that day, 'the Spirit and the Bride say, "Come"' (Rev. 22:17).

CONCLUSION

While this study is in many ways merely seminal, I am confident that the basic thesis I have proposed is true. More could be said, and undoubtedly further nuances and clarifications will be necessary. However, my primary concern is that, while particulars of what I have written may need revision and even correction, the core of what I have submitted conforms with and, indeed, advances the central tradition of the Church of both East and West. This confidence is founded upon the belief that this study is thoroughly biblical in origin and execution, and that it is creatively faithful to the received tradition of the Church. Moreover, because of these two factors, I believe this work is truly ecumenical, and my hope and prayer is that it will help foster unity between the Orthodox and the Catholic Churches. Above all, I hope that this conception of the Trinity will engender among all Christians a new love for the Father who begets his Son in the Spirit and has allowed us to be begotten in that same Spirit so as to be adopted as his sons and daughters.

St. Augustine said of his own study of the Trinity: 'Nowhere else is a mistake more dangerous, or the search more laborious, or discovery more advantageous.'[1] The labor of this study has brought

---

[1]   *De Trinitate*, I:5.

joy, and what I have discovered has caused delight, and, should there be any mistakes, I will eagerly abandon them. The desire of my heart is to know only the truth and to glorify, in truth and love, the one God – the Father, the Son, and the Holy Spirit.

IS IT APPROPRIATE TO USE THE TERM 'PERSON' IN RELATION TO THE TRINITY?

A good deal of discussion is taking place among contemporary theologians on the suitability of designating as 'persons' the Father, the Son, and the Holy Spirit. This is not a new concern. The Cappadocians tried to distinguish between the *ousia* of God and the Father, the Son, and the Holy Spirit, and settled upon the use of the terms *hypostasis* or *prosopon*, that is, the concrete individual and subjective expression of the *ousia*.[1] Augustine, in his classic statement, concedes that we must use the term 'person' 'so that we are not simply reduced to silence when we are asked three what?'.[2]

Today's discussion of the term 'person' has arisen both on the trinitarian and christological levels. There is the trinitarian concern that the term 'person', when applied to the Father, the Son, and the Holy Spirit, either is inadequate or, worse still, imparts an erroneous connotation. Within our post-Lockean and post-Kantian milieu, does not three 'persons' imply three subjective individual consciousnesses,

---

[1] See Hanson, *The Search for the Christian Doctrine of God*, pp. 676–737.

[2] *De Trinitate*, VII:11. Augustine discusses the different vocabulary used by the East and the West and the inadequacy of human language when applied to the Trinity (see ibid., V: 9–10 and VII: 9–11).

and thus lead to tritheism when applied to God? On the christological level the debate has centered upon calling Jesus 'a divine person' – the eternal Son. If Jesus is a divine 'person', can he in any authentic sense be said to be fully human – a human person? The implications of the christological debate for trinitarian thought are readily apparent. If Jesus as the Son of God is not a divine 'person', then this seems to prevent the use of the term 'person', if not for the Father, at least for the Holy Spirit. Since this study has upheld the use of the term 'person' when applied to the Father, the Son, and the Holy Spirit, a brief explanation of the present concerns and an apology for using the term 'person', when applied to the Trinity, is in order here.

What is surprising, though it is itself the cause, is that this query about the use of the term 'person' has arisen at a time when theology has shown an intense interest in the notion of personhood and personalist philosophies. Within scriptural, systematic, moral, and spiritual theology, contemporary Christian thought and church teaching have emphasized the importance of human personhood. The sacred scriptures themselves and the Christian tradition, along with contemporary philosophy and psychology, have cultivated and kindled this revival of an authentically Christian and thoroughly human personalism.[3] However, it is precisely this preoccupation with human personalism that has given rise to the christological and trinitarian issues. Since these two issues intersect at the point of

---

[3] For a few examples of this renewed emphasis on the concept of person within contemporary philosophy and theology, see Fatula, *The Triune God of Christian Faith*; Gaybba, *The Spirit of Love*; J. Galot, *The Person of Christ* (Chicago: Franciscan Herald Press, 1983); A. Kelly, *The Trinity of Love*; Weinandy, *Does God Change?*, pp. 88–100, 184–6; K. Wojtyla, *The Acting Person* (London: D. Reidel Publishing Company, 1979); Zizioulas, *Being as Communion*.

For the development of the concept of 'person' within Patristic thought, see O'Donnell, *The Mystery of the Triune God*, pp. 100–11; Prestige, *God in Patristic Thought*; Joseph Ratzinger, 'Concerning the Notion of Person in Theology', *Communio* 17 (Fall, 1990) 439–54; Stead, *Divine Substance*.

Jesus' identity, they are intimately related. We will first examine the christological concerns since it is here that the question is most acute and that the battle is won or lost as far as speaking of a trinity of persons is concerned.

The historical Jesus is the locus of our trinitarian faith. Christians believe that in him God manifested himself in a unique way as Son. Thus, in turn, Jesus revealed God to be our Father. Moreover, as a result of his death and resurrection, Jesus as Lord has been empowered by the Father to send forth the Spirit as the first gift to those who believe. As a consequence of the doctrinal development of this biblical faith, some contemporary theologians detect both linguistic and conceptual difficulties.[4]

Christological Concerns

Many contemporary christologists argue that to profess that Jesus is the eternal, divine person of the Son existing as man jeopardizes his true and full humanity. To define personhood, as we commonly do today, as the possessing of a subjective and unique personality, with the corresponding attributes of self-consciousness and freedom, seems to demand that Jesus be a human person. However, if Jesus is a divine person, with a divine subjectivity, personality, and self-consciousness, he cannot, it is asserted, equally be a human person. The divine person usurps or, at least, diminishes Jesus' human personhood. Yet both scripture and the orthodox tradition demand that Jesus be thoroughly human. When we examine the scriptural portrayal of Jesus, do we not perceive a human person speaking,

---

[4] Historically this revelation gave rise to a Christology and a trinitarian theology that has been conceived and articulated in terms of 'persons' and 'natures'. Traditional systematic theology taught and conciliar statements defined that Jesus was (and is) the one person (*prosopon, hypostasis, persona*) of the Son existing in two natures (*ousiai, physes, naturae*) – one divine and one human. The Trinity is the one divine substance/being (*ousia, physis, natura, essentia, substantia*) of God existing in three persons (*prosopa, hypostases, personae*). It is this articulation that has presently come into question.

teaching, suffering, and dying?

In order to rescue the authentic humanity of Jesus contemporary Christology often resorts to either of two solutions which frequently blend together. The first is some form of 'adoptionism', according to which Jesus' relationship to God differs in degree from our own relationship with God and does not differ in kind.[5] Here the human person of Jesus uniquely embodies or incarnates some aspect of God's immanent presence in the world, such as the spirit of love or the word of truth. In speaking God's full word Jesus manifests that he is the revelational expression of God's inner truth. In his selfless redemptive suffering and death he manifests his loyal and obedient sonship, and so demonstrates God's inner stance of love on behalf of humankind. This form of adoptionism is primarily epistemological or revelational in nature. In and through his words and deeds the human person of Jesus manifested his filial relationship to the Father and the Father in turn used Jesus as his human medium of revelation.

Within contemporary expressions of adoptionism, as within its ancient forms, God is normally understood to be one person – one personal, subjective being – who expresses and reveals himself through a human agent – a human person. However, unlike the motivation of early adoptionists, such as the Ebionites and Paul of

---

[5] For some examples of this trend within Christology see Donald Cupitt, *The Debate about Christ* (London: SCM, 1979); John Hick (ed.), *The Myth of God Incarnate* (London: SCM, 1977); John Hick, *The Metaphor of God Incarnate* (London: SCM, 1993); Elizabeth Johnson, *Consider Jesus: Waves of Renewal in Christology* (New York: Crossroad, 1990); John Knox, *The Humanity and Divinity of Christ* (Cambridge: Cambridge University Press, 1967); Hans Küng, *On Being a Christian* (Garden City: Doubleday, 1976); James Mackey, *Jesus: The Man and the Myth* (New York: Paulist Press, 1979); John Macquarrie, *Jesus Christ in Modern Thought* (London: SCM, 1990); Gerald O'Collins, *What Are They Saying About Jesus?* (New York: Paulist Press, 1977); J.A.T. Robinson, *The Human Face of God* (London: SCM, 1973); Piet Schoonenberg, *The Christ* (London: Sheed & Ward, 1971); William Thompson, *The Jesus Debate: A Survey and Synthesis (New York: Paulist Press, 1985).*

Some forms of 'Spirit' Christology are also adoptionistic in character. See G.W.H. Lampe, *God As Spirit* (Oxford: Clarendon Press, 1977); Roger Haight, 'The Case for Spirit Christology', *Theological Studies* 53 (1992) 257–87.

Samosata, who wanted to protect the oneness of God, contemporary adoptionists wish to preserve the full humanity of Jesus, yet in both instances the Trinity, by necessity, vanishes.

We find within contemporary Process Theology and its variants a more metaphysical approach to the Incarnation, and one that attempts to preserve, at least among some authors, a trinitarian view of God.[6] Unlike the traditional view of God as *actus purus* or *ipsum esse*, and thus immutable and impassible, Process thought desires to envision God in a way that is more personal and inter-relational, and thus more in keeping with biblical revelation – a God who is intimately and necessarily enmeshed in the actual developing world of persons – their hopes and joys, their pain and suffering. Thus God is here perceived as a changing and maturing participant in the ongoing process of all reality and of the historical, evolutionary order.

God then, within Process thought, by making present his infinite potential, lures or persuades human persons to actualize his latent good and value which he, in turn, takes into his concrete existing nature. Metaphysically this is worked out in the Process notion of 'prehension'. At each moment a person (or actual entity) prehends, that is, concretizes in his or her personal existence, some of God's potential good, thus allowing God to prehend it into his own personal concrete existence. This is the 'eternal' circle of reality's process.

Reinterpreting the Christian gospel from within the framework of Process Theology, Process theologians speak of the good or value by which God lures human persons as the Logos, that is, God's ever-present word, reason, or aim. The Logos is God going out of himself into the concrete world so as to be historically incarnated by human beings. The human person of Jesus, as *the* Word or Logos of God,

---

[6] For examples of Process Christology, see David Griffin, *A Process Christology* (Philadelphia: Westminster Press, 1973); Schubert Ogden, *The Reality of God* (New York: Harper and Row, 1966); Schubert Ogden, *The Point of Christology* (London: SCM, 1982); Norman Pittenger, *Christology Reconsidered* (London: SCM, 1970).

incarnated the aims or purposes of God to the greatest degree. As Son of God Jesus fully personalized the Word or Logos of God. Thus he becomes the paradigm or archetype of all Christian living. In his person he manifested what life is all about. He uniquely made present, in a thoroughly human, personal manner, the essence of all that God is up to in the world and in people's lives. Many Process theologians believe that such an understanding both preserves the full divinity of Jesus and equally rescues and guarantees his full humanity. Jesus was an authentic human person thoroughly incarnating the Logos of God in the world. Likewise, the trinitarian, or at least a binitarian, notion of God is preserved.[7]

Elsewhere I have addressed the question of Jesus' divinity in relation to his full and complete humanity, as well as the philosophical and theological adequacy of Process Christology.[8] However, I wish to argue here that, while Jesus is the eternal Son of the Father, and therefore a divine person or subject, this in no way undermines the full integrity of his humanity. Jesus is a full human person in the contemporary sense, that is, possessing a human self-consciousness, with all its concomitant attributes, such as freedom. Jesus possesses a human 'I'. What the Incarnation demands, and the Councils have defined and the tradition has articulated, is that the identity (the

---

[7]   Despite its claims of preserving and articulating a scriptural view of God in keeping with the best of the Christian tradition, Process Theology is reminiscent of, and in almost complete identity with, Neo-Platonism. God is but the Logos principle who orders reality. What distinguishes Process Theology is its Hegelian turn toward a cosmic process in which God is also a maturing member. Process Theology simply conceives the Logos as the impersonal emanation of God into the world only to be personified in a rational being. Even if Process Theology, similar to the Apologists of the second and third centuries, did conceive of the Logos as a person in and of himself, he would nonetheless be economically subordinate to the Father and not possess a distinct subjectivity inherent within the very nature of God's inner being.

[8]   See Weinandy, *Does God Change?* especially pp. 124–53, and *In the Likeness of Sinful Flesh.*

who) of this human 'I' be the eternal Son. If the human 'I' is not identified as God the Son, then no true incarnation has taken place. If the subject (the who) of the human 'I' is not the divine Son, then Jesus differs from us in his relationship to God only in degree and not in kind. (He does not differ from us in his humanity, which is *homoousios* with our own.)

What must principally be noted for present purposes is that this human 'I' is that of a divine subject. If the human 'I' is not identified with the divine subject, if the human 'I' only gives personal expression to some impersonal facet or aspect of God's being in the world, it would mean that in the 'incarnation' (the greatest expression of God in our midst) God would be less than a person. Only if the Son actually identifies himself with − so as to be ontologically one with − a human 'I', does the Son reveal that he is at least equal to our greatest dignity, that is, existing as persons.

While we may not fathom the fullness of what it means for the Father, the Son, and the Holy Spirit to be persons, we know that in the Incarnation the Son is a divine subject or person in a way that is analogous to and compatible with our own dignity as persons or subjects. The Son, as a divine subject, may be more than we are as persons, but he is not less than we are as persons, and we know this because the divine and eternal Son, in the Incarnation, has now identified himself with a human 'I'. The human 'I' of Jesus reveals the personhood or subjectivity of the eternal Son, for the Son's identity is one with that 'I'. Thus, human personhood is the prerequisite for a fully adequate revelation of the very nature of God as a trinity of divine persons or subjects in that one of the persons (the Son) has now identified himself with a human 'I'.

Much of contemporary Christology does not adequately address Rahner's concern that present-day Christianity is insufficiently trinitarian. Rather it reinforces the problem by proposing solutions that are either religiously or philosophically monotheistic in nature.

Trinitarian Concerns

On the trinitarian level, the term 'person' seems to imply, again using our contemporary psychological understanding of person, three people or at best three distinct and individual subjects with their own separate (and not just distinct) subjectivity, consciousness and freedom. This would verge on tritheism: three gods. There have been various attempts to surmount these difficulties in an orthodox manner.

Karl Rahner and Karl Barth have both questioned the suitability of the term 'person' for the above reason; that is, the term 'person' when applied to the Trinity implies today three people. Rahner argues that it would be better to speak of the one God as subsisting in three distinct manners.[9] Barth speaks in terms of God existing in three distinct modes.[10] Both theologians obviously wish to remain faithful to the truth of Christian revelation, but while such language frees the Christian faith from any form of tritheism, it places it very close to Sabellianism or Modalism. The Father, and more especially the Son and the Holy Spirit, tend to lose their own intra-trinitarian identity and subjectivity. It is ironic that Rahner, after forthrightly censuring the Christian tradition for being practically monotheistic, has himself proposed a solution that is, in many respects, only verbally or symbolically trinitarian.[11]

---

[9]   See Rahner, *The Trinity*, pp. 103–20.

[10]   See K. Barth, *Church Dogmatics*, I/1 (Edinburgh: T&T Clark, 1956), p. 412.

[11]   Kasper comments on Rahner and Barth:

> It must in fact be said that if the concept of person is open to misunderstanding, the concept of 'distinct manner of subsistence' is unintelligible ... And nowadays is not modalism or weak theism a far greater danger than the tritheism which Barth and Rahner conjure up? (*The God of Jesus Christ*, p. 288).

Moltmann calls Rahner's proposal 'Idealistic Modalism' and states that his

Here again we detect the importance of maintaining the term 'person' both when speaking of the divinity of Jesus and, consequently, when speaking of the Father, the Son and the Holy Spirit. By specifying that the identity of the historical Jesus is actually the person of the eternal Son, we not only preserve the truth of the Incarnation, but we equally confirm the basis for an authentic understanding of the Trinity as well. Conferring upon Jesus a personal identity that is divine establishes the truth that the inner being of God consists of three subjective 'whos' each possessing their own unique subjectivity and irreducible identity.[12]

Granted that the contemporary notion of 'person' as a subjective self-conscious, autonomous, free individual must be nuanced when applied to the Trinity, the specifically modern insistence that personhood necessarily implies unique subjectivity is actually an advantage, and not a hindrance, to our present understanding of the Trinity. The stress on subjectivity better enables us today to grasp that within the inner being of God there are truly three subjects and not three impersonal 'things'. It further deepens and clarifies, it radically 'personalizes' for our time and culture, the traditional

---

'reinterpretation of the doctrine of the Trinity ends in the mystic solitariness of God. It obscures the history of the Father, the Son, and the Holy Spirit to which the Bible testifies, by making this the eternal illustration of the inner experience. Is there really any "greater danger" than this "modalism"?' (*The Trinity and the Kingdom of God*, p. 148; see also pp. 139–48).

For an excellent critique of Rahner see G. Havrilak, 'Karl Rahner and the Greek Trinity', *St Vladimir's Theological Quarterly* 34/1 (1990) 61–77. See also de Margerie, *The Christian Trinity in History*, pp. 212–21; O'Donnell, *The Mystery of the Triune God*, pp. 102–6; L. Porter, 'On Keeping "Persons" in the Trinity: A Linguistic Approach to Trinitarian Thought', *Theological Studies* 41 (1980) 534–48.

[12] Von Balthasar states that only the Incarnation makes the Trinity accessible to us. 'This provides the last and decisive vindication of the principle we have been setting forth in this book, namely, that theological persons cannot be defined in isolation from their dramatic action. We know about the Father, Son and Spirit as divine "Persons" only through the figure and disposition of Jesus Christ' (*Theo-Drama*, Vol. III, p. 508; see also p. 511).

Scholastic notion of person as an individual substance of a rational nature. Rightly, the emphasis is now fixed upon subjectivity and not on substance.[13] Thus, to say that there are three persons in God may not do full, or even adequate, justice to the truth of who God is, but it would be deceptive and wrong to say anything less.[14]

----

[13] I would hold that 'consciousness' does not apply to the one common *ousia* or *substantia* of God, but to the three persons. While there is one consciousness in God, it is not shared generically by the Father, the Son, and the Holy Spirit. Rather each person defines and specifies this one consciousness in their own distinct manner. The Father possesses the divine consciousness in a manner that is peculiar to being the Father, and likewise the Son and the Holy Spirit. To deny that each person of the Trinity subsists with their own distinct consciousness would be to deny their distinct and irreducible personhood. They subsist in relation to one another, and their individual consciousness of one another and the whole of their mutual divinity defines their relational subsistence. As Kasper writes:

> We have no choice, then, but to say that in the Trinity we are dealing with three subjects who are reciprocally conscious of each other by reason of one and the same consciousness which the three subjects 'possess', each in his own proper way (*The God of Jesus Christ*, p. 289; see also pp. 285–90).

See also Gaybba, *The Spirit of Love*, pp. 120–4; W. Hill, *The Three-Personed God*, pp. 262–72; O'Donnell, *The Mystery of the Triune God*, p. 109–11.

[14] Aquinas is absolutely correct when he states that we can rightly use the term 'person' when applied to the Father, the Son, and the Holy Spirit for ' "person" signifies what is most perfect in all nature' (*S.T.*, I, 29, 3).
Kasper writes:

> It is obvious, of course, that we can apply the category of person to God only by analogy. This does not mean that God is less a person than we are, but rather that he is a person in an incomparably higher way than we are. But the statement that God is a person in an incomparably higher way than we are is to be distinguished from the thesis that God is supra-personal. When all is said and done, this thesis really says nothing, because 'person' is the highest category we have at our disposal. We can predicate the category in an analogous way, but to try to move beyond it into a higher, supra-personal dimension would mean leaving behind the realm of meaningful and responsible language. God's essence would then

The present study shows that the term 'person' not only establishes and guarantees the authentic individuality of the Father, the Son, and the Holy Spirit as well as their unity of nature, but also does so in a manner that exceeds and deepens the traditional understanding. Each person of the Trinity is active, including the Holy Spirit, and so is constitutive of the subjectivity of the other two as they mutually subsist as distinct subjects or persons in relation to one another. Moreover, it is this personalism that is the fundamental and constitutive basis of our own relationship, we who are persons, with the Trinity. For the ultimate ground of our life, the source and fulfillment of our happiness, both finite and eternal, to be less than personal would be demeaning rather than enhancing.

---

disappear into utter vagueness, indeterminacy and generality. This would be to misunderstand the biblical God, who has a concrete name.

The category of person has three positive values:

1. The category of person holds fast to the truth that God is not an object or thing that can be observed and thus pinned down; he is, instead, a subject that exists, speaks and acts in freedom which cannot be reduced to anything else . . .

2. The category of person holds fast to the truth that God is not a predicate either of the world or of man; it emphasizes the fact that God is a sovereign subject . . .

3. The category of person not only asserts the existence of God as a unique subject; it also says that God is the reality which determines everything . . . When we define God, the reality that determines everything, as personal we are also defining being as a whole as personal. This entails a revolution in the understanding of being. The ultimate and highest reality is not substance but relation (*The God of Jesus Christ*, pp. 155–6).

Zizioulas, in his excellent study on the notion of 'person', argues forcefully for Kasper's last point. See *Being as Communion*, pp. 27–65. See also Porter, 'On Keeping "Persons" in the Trinity', pp.530–48, especially pp. 547–8; and A. Kelly, *The Trinity of Love*, pp. 184–9.

EXCURSUS TWO:

THE IMMANENT AND THE
ECONOMIC TRINITY:
A RESPONSE TO LACUGNA[1]

In her major study on the Trinity *(God For Us: The Trinity and Christian Life)* Catherine Mowry LaCugna contends that theology should abandon the distinction between the immanent and the economic Trinity as it has been understood within contemporary theology. She believes that such a distinction segregates 'God in himself' from 'God for us', and so fixes a gap between them, rendering God irrelevant to the Christian life. In contrast, LaCugna proposes, and this is the theme of her entire book, that the whole trinitarian enterprise must be executed within a soteriological context.[2]

However, since the Council of Nicea the history of the development of the doctrine of the Trinity has focused, both in the East and in the West, on the immanent Trinity and the intradivine relationships between the persons. This is especially true of Latin trinitarian theology, where Augustine and Aquinas founded their trinitarian conception on the notion of substance and articulated a

---

[1]   This Excursus was first published in slightly different form as an article: 'The Immanent and Economic Trinity', *The Thomist* 57/4 (1993) 655–66.

[2] See *God For Us*, pp. 15, 211.

trinity of persons who are enclosed upon one another.[3] The more theology articulated and so developed the doctrine of the immanent Trinity, the more the doctrine of the Trinity became irrelevant. LaCugna completes her lengthy, and often insightful, study of the historical development of the doctrine of the Trinity by concluding: 'The history of doctrine and theology tells the story of the emergence and defeat of the doctrine of the Trinity.'[4]

Even if one argues, as Rahner and many othes including myself do, that the immanent Trinity *is* the economic Trinity, a gulf is still placed between God as he exists in himself and the God who exists for us.[5] There remains, according to LaCugna, a separation between *theologia*, that is, knowledge and speculation about God *qua* God, and *oikonomia*, that is, knowledge and speculation about God-for-us. For LaCugna, if *theologia* is to be relevant by being inherently and thoroughly soteriological, *theologia* can only be *theologia* of the *oikonomia*; that is, a theology of God's action within the world. A *theologia* of the Trinity must then be a *theologia* of the trinitarian self-

---

[3]   With reference to the Western conception of the Trinity in contrast to that of the East, LaCugna comments:

> However, the economy of salvation *a Patre ad Patrem* becomes all the harder to see once the consubstantiality of persons is situated in the intradivine domain, or beyond, in a permanently unknowable and imparticipable divine essence. (ibid., p. 73).

For comments on how Augustine's trinitarian thought brought about a rupture between God in himself and God for us see pp. 80, 91, 97, 101–2, 104. For a similar criticism of Aquinas see pp. 157, 167–8.

[4]   Ibid., p. 198. Cf., pp. 209–10, 392.

[5]   LaCugna gives a clear exposition of Rahner's position on the distinction and relationship between the immanent and the economic Trinity (ibid., pp. 211–21). She concludes: 'Finally, according to Rahner at least, distinctions in the economy originate in and are grounded in distinctions "in" God. It is on the last point that we part ways with Rahner' (p. 211).

expression within the *oikonomia*, as God has revealed himself within the economy. Her governing principle is: '*theologia* is fully revealed and bestowed in *oikonomia*, and *oikonomia* truly expresses the ineffable mystery of *theologia*.'[6]

> [The economy is not] a mirror dimly reflecting a hidden realm of intradivine relations; the economy is God's concrete existence in Christ and as Spirit. The economy is the 'distribution' of God's life lived with and for the creature. Economy and theology are two aspects of *one* reality: the mystery of divine-human communion.[7]

Thus the Trinity that is revealed is not a Trinity apart or distinct from the economy, but a Trinity of the economy. 'The referent for the immanent Trinity is not "God *in se*", or "God's essence as it is in itself". Theories about what God is apart from God's self-communication in salvation history remain unverifiable and ultimately untheological, since *theologia* is given only through *oikonomia*.'[8]

---

[6] Ibid., p. 221.

[7] Ibid., p. 222.

[8] Ibid., p. 231. See also pp. 224–8. For LaCugna theology fell to the temptation to seek to articulate the inner life of God: 'to find reasons for the coequality of persons in an independent metaphysics rather than in the record of the economy, and, to confuse the immanent structure of salvation history with the "inner life" of God. As we have seen, the notion of God's "inner life" simply cannot stand up to scrutiny' (p. 229).
  LaCugna is in basic agreement with Schoonenberg that we are incapable of moving from the Trinity as revealed in the economy to speculation about the Trinity as it may exist in itself. We do not know whether God actually exists as a Trinity apart from God's trinitarian expression in the economy. All we know is the economic expression. 'This is the import of Schoonenberg's point that the question of whether God would be trinitarian apart from salvation history is purely speculative and cannot be answered on the basis of revelation' (p. 227; see also pp. 217–20, and p. 236, n. 21).

LaCugna therefore argues:

> There is neither an economic nor an immanent Trinity; there
> is only the *oikonomia* that is the concrete realization of the
> mystery of *theologia* in time, space, history, and personality.
> In this framework, the doctrine of the Trinity encompasses
> much more than the immanent Trinity, envisioned in static
> ahistorical and transeconomic terms; the subject matter of
> the Christian theology of God is the one dynamic movement
> of God, *a Patre ad Patrem* ... The existence of such an
> intradivine realm is precisely what cannot be established
> on the basis of the economy, despite the fact that it has
> functioned within speculative theology ever since the late
> fourth century.

This revision of the basic trinitarian framework obviates
the need to adhere to the language of economic and
immanent Trinity. These terms are bound inextricably to
the framework that operates with a gap between *oikonomia*
and *theologia*. The revision – more accurately, the return to
the bibilical and pre-Nicene pattern of thought – suggests
not only that we abandon the misleading terms, economic
and immanent Trinity, but that we also clarify the meaning
of *oikonomia* and *theologia*. *Oikonomia* is not the Trinity *ad
extra* but the comprehensive plan of God reaching from

For Schoonenberg's own article see 'Trinity – the Consummated Covenant.
Theses on the Doctrine of the Trinitarian God', *Studies in Religion* 5 (1975–6) 111–
16.

Commenting on Schoonenberg's position that to say the immanent Trinity
is dissolved in the economic Trinity, as though the eternal Trinity first came into
existence in and through history, Kasper states: 'In eternity the distinctions between
the three persons would then at best be modal, and would become real only in
history' (*The God of Jesus Christ*, p. 276). For other critiques of Schoonenberg's position
see Boff, *Trinity and Society*, p. 114 and von Balthasar, *Theo-Drama*, Vol. III, p. 508.

creation to consummation, in which God and all creatures
are destined to exist together in the mystery of love and
communion. Similarly, *theologia* is not the Trinity *in se*, but,
much more modestly and simply, the mystery of God.[9]

Within the economy of salvation, then, God manifests himself
within a trinitarian pattern. In the form of a descending and
ascending parabola, God expresses himself through Christ in the
Spirit and so sweeps us up into himself though Christ in the Spirit.
'This chiastic model of emanation and return, *exitus* and *reditus*,
expresses the one ecstatic movement of God outward by which all
things originate from God through Christ in the power of the Holy
Spirit, and all things are brought into union with God and return to
God.'[10]

The heart of LaCugna's trinitarian theology is the notion that
'to be' is 'to be relational'. The whole history of trinitarian thought
is founded upon this principle.[11] However, the Trinity does not exist
as an intradivine set of persons who subsist in relation to one another.
That would once more divide *theologia* and *oikonomia*.[12] Rather God,
within the economy, is inherently relational in that through Christ
and in the Spirit he relates to us and so unites us to himself in

---

[9] *God for Us*, p. 223.

[10] Ibid.

[11] See ibid., p. 288 –92. LaCugna wishes, following Zizioulas, to lay claim
to the Cappadocian insight that personhood is constitutive of substance and not
vice versa (see ibid., pp. 244–50, 260–6).

[12] LaCugna writes: 'The goal of theology is not knowledge of God "as God
is in Godself" disjoined from God's manifestations in the economy; the goal of
theologia is knowledge of God, which is inseparable from who God is in God's
concrete existence in Christ and the Spirit' (ibid., p. 233; see also p. 334).

communion.[13] For God to be is for God to be relational.[14] Unlike the limited relatedness of human beings, 'to God belongs the sphere of infinite relatedness, infinite capacity for relationship, infinite actuality of relationship, both to past, present, and future reality.'[15]

To quote her again at length, LaCugna writes:

> The relational ontology in which all of reality is referred to its origin in personhood – if it were carried forward through the whole of dogmatic theology – would avert the separation of *theologia* and *oikonomia*. The trinitarian *oikonomia* is the personal self-expressing and concrete *existence* of God. The ontology proper to this understands being as being-in-relation, not being-in-itself. The economy is 'proof' that God is not being-by-itself but being-with-us. The sphere of God's being-in-relation is the economy of creation and redemption in which the totality of God's life is given. We have no direct or immediate access to God's being in-itself or by-itself ... The heart of *theologia*, as also of *oikonomia*, is therefore relationship, personhood, communion. The mysteries of human personhood and communion have their origin and destiny in God's personal existence. The histories

---

[13] LaCugna does not see the *perichoresis* as designating the inter-communion between intradivine persons.

> The starting point in the economy of redemption, in contrast to the intradivine starting point, locates *perichoresis* not in God's inner life but in the mystery of the one communion of all persons, divine as well as human. From this standpoint 'the divine dance' is indeed an apt image of persons in communion: not from an intradivine communion but for divine life as all creatures partake and literally exist in it (ibid., p. 274; see also pp. 270–8).

[14] For LaCugna, 'This relational ontology follows from the fundamental unity of *oikonomia* and *theologia*; God's To-Be is To-Be-in relationship, and God's being-in-relationship-to-us *is* what God is' (ibid., p. 250).

[15] Ibid., p. 292.

of divine and human personhood intersect in the economy that proceeds *a Patre ad Patrem*, through Christ in the unity of the Holy Spirit.[16]

LaCugna maintains, then, that 'In God alone is there a full correspondence between personhood and being, between *hypostasis* and *ousia*. God for us is who God is as God.'[17] Ultimately, then, it does not matter whether one uses the term 'person' for God 'in the singular or plural, we are not giving a description of the essence of God as it is in itself, but using a term that points beyond itself to the ineffability of God'.

[This is so because] the proper focus of theology is the concrete manifestation of God's personal reality revealed in the face of Jesus Christ and the activity of the Holy Spirit. It does not so much matter whether we say God is one person in three modalities, or one nature in three persons, since these two assertions can be understood in approximately the same way. What matters is that we hold on to the assertion that God is *personal*, and that therefore the proper subject matter of the doctrine of the Trinity is the encounter between divine and human persons in the economy of redemption.[18]

The reason I have outlined LaCugna's position at some length, predominantly using her own words, is that firstly, it challenges my own position on the relationship between the immanent and the economic Trinity. But secondly, and more particularly, LaCugna's stance, as a Christian view of God and his relation to us, is, I believe, fatally and disastrously flawed.

---

[16] Ibid., p. 246.

[17] Ibid., p. 305.

[18] Ibid., see pp. 300–4.

LaCugna is absolutely correct that the God who is must be God-for-us. There is no other. There is no ontological difference between what God is in himself and what God is for us. However, in order for there to be a God-for-us there must be '*a*' God.[19] In order for there to be a Trinity-for-us there must be *a* Trinity. While there is no ontological distinction between the immanent and the economic Trinity – the Trinity which expresses itself in the economy must be one and the same Trinity that exists in itself – yet there is an ontological distinction between God and all else that exists. The *oikonomia* is the realm where God, in all his wholly otherness as God – ontologically distinct from the *oikonomia* – is present and acts, and in the Incarnation actually abides, in the fullness of his wholly divine otherness, as man. For LaCugna, God, in his wholly ontologically distinct otherness as God, actually never is present to nor acts within the *oikonomia*. Rather God is reduced to the *oikonomia* itself so that we no longer live with God in his wholly otherness, but only experience a God who has receded into and subsists wholly within the ontological level of the *oikonomia* itself.[20]

---

[19] By speaking of 'a' God, I do not want to imply that God is one of many beings, but precisely the opposite. God must exist ontologically distinct from all that is not God. As Aquinas states: 'God is not contained in any genus'. See *S.T.*, I, 3, 6.

[20] LaCugna does speak of the ineffable mystery of God, that God is always more than we can know, but this apophatic knowledge of God is an apophasis of the *oikonomia* – those aspects of God which remain mysterious to us within the economy.

> There is no hidden God (*deus absconditus*) behind the God of revelation history, no possibility that God is in God's eternal mystery other than what God reveals Godself to be ... It must be emphasized that divine immanence is not equivalent to the 'economic' Trinity, nor is divine transcendence equivalent to the 'immanent' Trinity. God's transcendence is not God out of relationship to us. God is transcendent because God's nearness to us in history does not exhaust the ineffable mystery of God. *Both* immanence and transcendence must be predicated not just of *theologia* but also of *oikonomia*: God's mystery is grasped as transcendent precisely

While wanting to eliminate the gap between God and us, LaCunga has actually constructed a chasm between God and us that is now unbridgeable. We only come to experience and know the phenomenal God of the *oikonomia*, and never the noumenal God who actually exists in his wholly ontologically distinct otherness as God.[21]

Thus LaCugna so collapses the Trinity into the economy that the economy is no longer the realm in which the Trinity acts, but the only realm in which 'the Trinity' *is*. The *oikonomia* is no longer the realm in which the trinity of persons as they exist, in all their otherness, act, and so relate to us in all their otherness as distinct divine subjects, but the only realm in which the trinity of 'persons' actually exist. The Trinity does not exist ontologically distinct from the economy. 'The Trinity' ontologically is the economy. Thus the Trinity is not the persons of the Father, the Son, and the Holy Spirit acting in time and relating to us in history as they are in themselves, but merely an impersonal theological principle grounding,

_____

in the economy of salvation. Vice versa, the economic self-revelation of God in Christ is grasped, albeit obliquely, as the mystery of *theologia* itself. If we adhere to the principle that economy and theology belong together as two aspects of one mystery, then *the economy of salvation is as ineffable as is the eternal mystery of God (theologia)* (p. 322; see also pp. 322–35).

Von Balthasar comments on such a view as LaCugna's:

While, according to Christian faith, the economic Trinity assuredly appears as the interpretation of the immanent Trinity, it may not be identified with it, for the latter grounds and supports the former. Otherwise the immanent, eternal Trinity would threaten to dissolve into the economic; in other words, God would be swallowed up in the world process – a necessary stage, in this view, if he is fully to realize himself (*Theo-Drama*, Vol. III, p. 508).

[21] If God is not ontologically distinct and other than the *oikonomia*, one ends up with either a finite God or a 'Christian' expression of atheism, both of which, in the end, may be equivalent.

sustaining, and articulating our relation to 'God' and with one another. God is no longer a trinity of persons or subjects. The term 'trinity' now merely expresses the trinitarian pattern or mode of God's revelation as manifested through Christ and in the Spirit by which human persons (including Christ) are related to God.

Similarly, one can question, although I do not believe she wants to hold this position, whether God, for LaCugna, is ultimately nothing more than the philosophical principle, inherent within reality, which gives rise to human relations and expresses 'the more' contained within them.[22] God does not exist 'outside' the economy. He is the economy.

While LaCugna consistently speaks in personal and relational terms and wishes to found her trinitarian theology upon them, in Part Two of her book where she presents her own theology of the Trinity, she assiduously avoids using the terms, 'Father', 'Son', and 'Holy Spirit'. Instead she speaks of 'God', 'Christ', and 'Spirit'.[23] She does this, I believe, for two interconnected reasons. Firstly, the terms 'God', 'Christ', and 'Spirit', are more compatible with her reductionist view of the Trinity as existing only in the economy. God (as relational, and not necessarily as Father) expresses himself through Jesus as the Christ in the Spirit. Secondly, I believe that she avoids the term 'Father' not only because she believes that God could be equally called 'Mother', but even more, in light of the above, because the term 'Father' (or 'Mother' for that matter) implies a 'Son'.[24] She wants to avoid the term 'Son' because that immediately presupposes a subject, and one that might be construed as ontologically divine

---

[22] In this case LaCugna's notion of God would be similar to Hegel's 'Spirit', or Heidegger's and Tillich's 'Ground of Being', or Process Theology's 'Di-polar' God.

[23] See for example pp. 320, 356, 365, 378.

[24] For LaCugna's view that God could equally be called 'Mother' see ibid., pp. 267–70, 280, 303.

apart from the economy. She normally drops 'Holy' from Spirit because that traditionally implies a subject as well. By speaking of 'God', 'Christ', and 'Spirit', LaCugna can speak of the relationality of God without speaking of divine subjects. Christ and the Spirit are not divine subjects, *homoousios* with the Father, rather they express how God relates to and acts within the world. Human beings are the only real persons or subjects within LaCugna's relational ontology. The human subject of Jesus supremely embodies God's relatedness to us in the Spirit and so is the Christ. The Spirit specifies the manner in which God acts in Christ and in each of us, and so is called Spirit.[25]

Thus, while LaCugna maintains the dynamism and even beauty of relational language, the notion of personhood, at least the personhood and subjectivity of the Father, the Son, and the Holy Spirit, is abandoned. They are not divine subjects and therefore all that LaCugna says about our unity and communion with 'them' is vacuous.[26]

This becomes particularly evident when LaCugna states that all that is said about God being personal and relational is mere metaphor. 'The systematic theologian needs to keep in mind that every concept, whether it be "substance" or "relation", is fundamentally metaphorical, not a literal description of what is.'[27]

---

[25] See ibid., pp. 296–8.

[26] LaCugna's Chapter 9 on 'Trinity, Theology, and Doxology' is spiritually and aesthetically moving. However, because the Father, the Son and the Holy Spirit are no longer divine subjects in themselves, the praises that we sing are devoid of theological content and meaning. We end up singing our own praises as persons rather than glorying in the majesty and splendor of the triune God.

[27] Ibid., p. 359; see also p. 354. LaCugna refers the reader to her other articles (p. 369, n. 2): C.M. LaCugna and K. McDonnell, 'Returning from "The Far Country": Theses for a Contemporary Trinitarian Theology', *The Scottish Journal of Theology*, 41 (1988) 191–215, esp. 204–5, and also C.M. LaCugna, 'Re-Conceiving the Trinity as the Mystery of Salvation', *The Scottish Journal of Theology*, 38 (1985) 1–23.

Such a view substantiates the previous criticism that the use of trinitarian language merely expresses an impersonal theological or philosophical principle which governs and underlies reality.

Moreover, while LaCugna wishes her trinitarian theology to be thoroughly soteriological, Jesus as the Christ does not relate to God in a different kind of way than we do, but only in a different degree.[28] Therefore, Christ exemplifies and embodies, and so reveals, how all of us relate to God in the Spirit. The actions of Christ and the Spirit do not, then, change our relationship with God in kind, but only in degree inasmuch as, because the pattern (trinitarian) is now manifest, we become consciously aware of it.[29]

LaCugna believes that her understanding of the Trinity is biblical and follows the pre-Nicene pattern; that is, that the Son and the Holy Spirit are conceived primarily as the manner in which God acts within the economy.[30] The Son and Spirit emanate out from God only in relation to the economy of salvation – within creation and redemption. As the above shows, she believes such a notion sustains her premise that *theologia* and *oikonomia* are one and the same.

Now the pre-Nicene Fathers, as witnessed primarily in the Apologists, did stress the economic expression of the Trinity. The Son and the Spirit became distinct subjects emanating out from the Father only at creation and in redemption. This conception was due to their heavy reliance on Middle Platonic thought. However, the whole thrust of the pre-Nicene development was away from such a

---

[28] LaCugna denies that Jesus' sonship differs in kind from our own, and also that as Son, he is an eternal divine person. See ibid., pp. 309, n. 67 and 317, n. 143.

[29] On how Jesus, through his death and resurrection, changes our relationship with God not only in degree but in kind see Weinandy, *In the Likeness of Sinful Flesh.*

[30] See *God For Us*, pp. 221–3.

conception in the light of the biblical data and the Christian faith that grew out of it. We see this development already in Irenaeus, who pushed the economic expression of the Trinity well into the immanent nature of God. More and more, as witnessed in such theologians as Tertullian in the West and especially Origen in the East, the question of concern was how to conceive of God in such a manner as to uphold the oneness of God and yet allow that the Son and the Holy Spirit are eternal subjects within that oneness. The subordinationism and emanationism contained in the early Fathers were not expressions of their disbelief in the eternal divinity of the Son and the Spirit, nor expressions of a belief that the Son and the Spirit were only 'God' within the economy, but not 'God' apart from the economy; rather these were conceptual struggles and attempts to say exactly that – that the Son and the Spirit were God both within the being of God and within the economy of salvation. In a way, the pre-Nicene Fathers did not really want to say what they said, but could not express their ideas in any better way. LaCugna, on the contrary, does want to say what they said because she believes this is the best way to express it.

Actually, LaCugna's pre-Nicene version of the Trinity is not pre-Nicene at all. The pre-Nicene Fathers, including the Apologists, conceived the Son and the Spirit to be distinct divine subjects in themselves, at least within the economy; whereas LaCugna deprives them of their divine subjectivity even within the economy. The Son and the Spirit are only impersonal expressions of God's relatedness which becomes personified in human persons, including Christ. Thus, LaCugna's trinitarian theology is thoroughly Neo-Platonic and emanationist in character.

LaCugna believes that trinitarian theology took the wrong turn at the Council of Nicea. Nicea created 'the gap between *oikonomia* and *theologia*'.[31] By proclaiming the Son to be *homoousios* with the Father, Nicea compelled theology to speculate about the intradivine

[31] Ibid, p. 35; see also pp. 209, 231.

trinity of persons separate from the economy, rather than grasp that 'the Trinity' is entirely God's expression of himself within the economy. While she recognizes that Nicea is a stumbling-block to her trinitarian thought, LaCugna does not perceive its radical significance. It is Nicea that guarantees that the God we have come to know is truly the God who is *for us*.[32] Nicea forges the unbreakable ontological link between the economic and the immanent Trinity, and it does so by declaring that the one who is *wholly within* the economy is the same one who is *wholly other than* the economy. The Son, who is *homoousios* with the Father, and thus wholly God as the Father is God in all his wholly ontologically distinct otherness, is the same Son who became man, suffered under Pontius Pilate, was crucified, died and was buried. LaCugna's venture ultimately runs aground on the rock of *homoousios*.[33]

---

[32] The title of LaCugna's book is not without significance. While the book is on the Trinity, it is entitled *God For Us*. The reason is that the Father, the Son, and the Holy Spirit do not truly exist as divine subjects – only God exists, and thus it is he who is for us. He is 'for us' by expressing himself in a trinitarian pattern.

[33] Kasper is entirely correct when he states:

> There is at least one case in which this identity of economic and immanent Trinity is a defined truth of faith: the incarnation of the Logos, or hypostatic union . . . In the case of the incarnation, then, the temporal sending of the Logos into the world and his eternal procession from the Father cannot be completely distinguished; here immanent Trinity and economic Trinity form a unity (*The God of Jesus Christ*, pp. 274–5).

SELECT
BIBLIOGRAPHY

Anselm, St., *Basic Writings,* trans. S. Deane. LaSalle, IL: Open Court, 1968.

Athanasius, St., *Selected Writings and Letters.* Nicene and Post-Nicene Fathers, Second Series, Vol. 4. Reprinted Edinburgh: T&T Clark, 1987.

Augustine, St., *On the Trinity*, ed. & trans. E. Hill. Brooklyn: New City Press, 1991.

Barth, K., *Church Dogmatics.* Edinburgh: T&T Clark, 1956.

Boff, L., *The Trinity and Society.* New York: Orbis Books, 1988.

Bolotov, B., 'Thesen über das Filioque', *Revue Internationale de Théologie* 24 (1898) 271–89.

Bouyer, L., *Le Consolateur: Esprit Saint et Vie De Grace.* Paris: Les Editions du Cerf, 1980.

Bracken, J., *What Are They Saying About the Trinity?* New York: Paulist Press, 1979.

The Triune Symbol: Persons, Process and Community. Lanham, MD: University Press of America, 1985.

The British Council of Churches Study Commission, *The Forgotten Trinity.* London: Inter-Church House, 1989.

Brown, D., *The Divine Trinity.* LaSalle, IL: Open Court, 1985.

Brown, R., *The Birth of the Messiah*. New York: Doubleday, 1977.

Bulgakov, S., *Le Paraclet*. Paris: Aubier, 1946.

Clément, O., *L'Église Orthodoxe*. Paris: 1961.

    The Roots of Christian Mysticism. London: New City, 1993.

Coakley, S., 'Can God be Experienced as Trinity?', *The Modern Churchman* NS 28 (1986) 11–23.

Coakley, S. & Pailin, D. (eds), *The Making and Remaking of Christian Doctrine: Essays in Honour of Maurice Wiles*. Oxford: Clarendon Press, 1993.

Coffey, D., *Grace: The Gift of the Holy Spirit*. Sydney: Catholic Institute of Sydney, 1979.

    'The "Incarnation" of the Holy Spirit in Christ', *Theological Studies* 45 (1984) 466–80.

    'A Proper Mission of the Holy Spirit', *Theological Studies* 47 (1986) 227–50.

    'The Holy Spirit as the Mutual Love of the Father and the Son', *Theological Studies* 51 (1990) 193–229.

Congar, Y., *I Believe in the Holy Spirit*, 3 Vols. New York: Seabury Press, 1983.

    The Word and the Spirit. London: Geoffrey Chapman, 1986.

Cupitt, D., *The Debate About Christ*. London: SCM, 1979.

de Halleux, A., 'Orthodoxie et Catholicisme: du personnalisme en pneumatologie' *Revue Théologique de Louvain* 6 (1975) 13–14.

de la Taille, M., *The Hypostatic Union and Created Actuation by Uncreated Act*. West Baden Springs, IN: West Baden College, 1952.

de Margerie, B., *The Christian Trinity in History*. Petersham, MA: St. Bede's Publications, 1982.

Dunn, J.D.G., *Jesus and the Spirit*. London: SCM, 1975.

    Christology in the Making. Philadelphia: Westminster Press, 1980.

Durrwell, F.X., *Holy Spirit of God*. London: Geoffrey Chapman, 1986.

Evans, E. (ed), *Tertullian's Treatise Against Praxeas*. London: SPCK, 1948.

Evdokimov, P., *L'Esprit Saint dans la Tradition Orthodoxe*. Paris: Les Editions du Cerf, 1969.

Fatula, M.A., *The Triune God of Christian Faith*. Collegeville: The Liturgical Press, 1990.

Forte, B., *The Trinity as History*. New York: Alba House, 1989.

Fortman, E.J., *Theological Resources: The Triune God*. London: Hutchinson, 1972.

Galot, J., *The Person of Christ*. Chicago: Franciscan Herald Press, 1983.

Garrigues, J.-M., *L'Esprit Qui Dit 'Père!': L'Esprit-Saint dans la Vie Trinitaire et le Problème du Filioque*. Paris: Téqui, 1981.

Gaybba, B., *The Spirit of Love*. London: Geoffrey Chapman, 1987.

Griffin, D., *A Process Christology*. Philadelphia: Westminster Press, 1973.

Gunton, C., *Enlightenment and Alienation: An Essay Towards a Trinitarian Theology*. London: Marshall, Morgan and Scott, 1985.

The Promise of Trinitarian Theology. Edinburgh: T&T Clark, 1991.

The One, the Three and the Many: God, Creation and the Culture of Modernity. Cambridge: Cambridge University Press, 1993.

Haight, R., 'The Case for Spirit Christology', *Theological Studies* 53 (1992) 257–87.

Hanson, R.P.C., *The Search for the Christian Doctrine of God*. Edinburgh: T&T Clark, 1988.

Hardy, E. (ed), *Oratio Catechetica Magna*, 2, trans. from *Christology of the Later Fathers*. Philadelphia: Westminster Press, 1954.

Havrilak, G., 'Karl Rahner and the Greek Trinity', *St Vladimir's Theological Quarterly* 34/1 (1990) 61–77.

Heron, A., '"Who Proceedeth from the Father and the Son": The Problem of the Filioque', *Scottish Journal of Theology* 24 (1971) 149–66.

The Holy Spirit. Philadelphia: Westminster Press, 1983.

Hick, J. (ed), *The Myth of God Incarnate.* London: SCM, 1977.

The Metaphor of God Incarnate. London: SCM, 1993.

Hill, E., *The Mystery of the Trinity.* London: Geoffrey Chapman, 1985.

Hill, W., *The Three-Personed God.* Washington, D.C.: Catholic University of America Press, 1982.

Hopkins, J., *A Companion to the Study of St. Anselm.* Minneapolis: University of Minnesota Press, 1972.

Jensen, R., *The Triune Identity.* Philadelphia: Fortress Press, 1982.

Jeremias, J., *The Prayers of Jesus.* London: SCM, 1967.

Johnson, E., *Consider Jesus: Waves of Renewal in Christology.* New York: Crossroad, 1990.

Jüngel, E., *The Doctrine of the Trinity: God's Being is in Becoming.* Grand Rapids, MI: Eerdmans, 1976.

Kasper, W., *The God of Jesus Christ.* New York: Crossroad, 1986.

Jesus the Christ. New York: Paulist Press, 1976

Kelly, A., *The Trinity of Love.* Wilmington: Michael Glazier, 1989.

Kelly, J.N.D., *Early Christian Doctrines.* London: A. & C. Black, 1968, 4th ed.

Knox, J., *The Humanity and Divinity of Christ.* Cambridge: Cambridge University Press, 1967.

Küng, H., *On Being a Christian.* Garden City: Doubleday, 1976.

Küng, H. & Moltmann, J. (eds), *Concilium: Conflicts About the Holy Spirit*, Vol. 128. New York: Seabury Press, 1979.

LaCugna, C.M., 'Re-Conceiving the Trinity as the Mystery of Salvation', *The Scottish Journal of Theology* 38 (1985) 1–23.

God For Us: The Trinity and Christian Life. San Francisco: Harper Collins, 1991.

LaCugna, C.M., & McDonnell, K., 'Returning from "The Far Country": Theses for a Contemporary Trinitarian Theology', *The Scottish Journal of Theology* 41 (1988) 191–215.

Lampe, G.W.H., *God As Spirit*. Oxford: Clarendon Press, 1977.

Laurentin, R., *The Truth of Christmas*. Petersham, MA: St. Bede's Publications, 1986.

Lossky, V., 'The Procession of the Holy Spirit in the Orthodox Triadology', *Eastern Churches Quarterly* 7 (1948) 31–52.
The Mystical Theology of the Eastern Church. London: James Clarke, 1957.

Mackey, J., *Jesus: The Man and the Myth*. New York: Paulist Press, 1979.
The Christian Experience of God as Trinity. London: SCM, 1983.

Macquarrie, J., *Jesus Christ in Modern Thought*. London: SCM, 1990.

Marsh, T., *The Triune God: A Biblical, Historical and Theological Study*. Blackrock, Dublin: Columba Press, 1994.

Martins, J.S., (ed), *Credo In Spiritum Sanctum: Atti Del Congresso Teologico Internazionale Di Pneumatologia*, 2 Vols. Rome: Libreria Editrice Vaticana, 1982.

Mascall, E.L., *The Triune God: An Ecumenical Study*. London: Churchman Publishing, 1986.

Massabki, C., *Who Is the Holy Spirit?* New York: Alba House, 1979.

Meyendorff, J., *Byzantine Theology*. New York: Fordham University Press, 1979.

Moltmann, J., *The Trinity and the Kingdom of God*. New York: Harper and Row, 1981.
History and the Triune God. London: SCM, 1991.
The Spirit of Life: A Universal Affirmation. London: SCM, 1992.

Mühlen, H., *Der Heilige Geist als Person*. (2nd edition) Münster: Aschendorff, 1967.

O'Collins, G., *What Are They Saying About Jesus?* New York: Paulist Press, 1977.

O'Donnell, J., *The Mystery of the Triune God*. New York: Paulist Press, 1989.

'In Him and Over Him: The Holy Spirit in the Life of Jesus', *Gregorianum* 70 (1989) 25–45.

Ogden, S., *The Reality of God*. New York: Harper and Row, 1966.

The Point of Christology. London: SCM, 1982.

Pannenberg, W., *Systematic Theology*, Vol. 1. Grand Rapids, MI: Eerdmans, 1991.

Pelikan, J., *The Christian Tradition: A History of the Development of Doctrine*. Vol. 1: *The Emergence of the Catholic Tradition (100–600)*. Chicago: Chicago University Press, 1971.

The Christian Tradition: A History of the Development of Doctrine. Vol. 2: *The Spirit of Eastern Christendom (600–1700)*. Chicago: Chicago University Press, 1974.

Peters, T., *God as Trinity*. Louisville: John Knox Press, 1993.

Pittenger, N., *Christology Reconsidered*. London: SCM, 1970.

Porter, L., 'On Keeping "Persons" in the Trinity: A Linguistic Approach to Trinitarian Thought', *Theological Studies* 41 (1980) 530–48.

Prestige, G.L., *God in Patristic Thought*. London: SPCK, 1952.

Rahner, K., *The Trinity*. New York: Herder and Herder, 1970.

Ratzinger, J., 'Concerning the Notion of Person in Theology', *Communio* 17 (1990) 439–54.

A Report by the Doctrine Commission of the General Synod of the Church of England, *We Believe in the Holy Spirit*. London: Church House Publishing, 1991.

Robinson, J.A.T., *The Human Face of God*. London: SCM, 1973.

Schillebeeckx, E., *Jesus, An Experiment in Christology*. New York: Seabury, 1979.

Schoonenberg, P., *The Christ*, London: Sheed & Ward, 1971.

'Trinity – the Consummated Covenant. Theses on the Doctrine

of the Trinitarian God', *Studies in Religion* 5 (1975–6) 111–16.

Schwöbel, C. & Gunton, C., (eds), *Persons, Divine and Human. King's College Essays in Theological Anthropology*. Edinburgh: T&T Clark, 1992.

Sherry, P., *Spirit and Beauty: An Introduction to Theological Aesthetics*. Oxford: Clarendon Press, 1992.

Smail, T., *The Forgotten Father*. London: Hodder & Stoughton, 1980.

Stead, C.G., 'The Origins of the Doctrine of the Trinity', *Theology* 77 (1974) 508–17, 582–9.

Divine Substance. Oxford: Clarendon Press, 1977.

Swete, H.B., *The Holy Spirit in the Ancient Church*. London: Macmillan, 1912.

Swinburne, R., *The Christian God*. Oxford: Clarendon Press, 1994

Taylor, J.V., *The Go-Between God: The Holy Spirit and the Christian Mission*. London: SCM, 1972.

Thomas Aquinas, St., *Summa Theologica*, trans. English Dominican Fathers. New York: Benziger Brothers, 1947.

Thompson, W., *The Jesus Debate: A Survey and Synthesis*. New York: Paulist Press, 1985.

Thurmer, J., *A Detection of the Trinity*. Exeter: Paternoster Press, 1984.

Toon P. & Spiceland, J. (eds), *One God in Trinity*. London: Samuel Bagster, 1980.

Torrance, T.F., *Theology in Reconciliation*. London: Geoffrey Chapman, 1975.

The Trinitarian Faith. Edinburgh: T&T Clark, 1988.

Trinitarian Perspectives: Toward Doctrinal Agreement. Edinburgh: T&T Clark, 1994.

Torrance, T.F., (ed), *Theological Dialogue Between Orthodox and Reformed Churches*, 2 Vols. Edinburgh: Scottish Academic Press, 1985 & 1993.

Vasilj, K., *Trinitarian Theories as Judged by Reason: A New Theory*. Chicago: Ziral, 1987.

Vischer, L. (ed), *Spirit of God, Spirit of Christ: Ecumenical Reflections on the Filioque Controversy*. London: SPCK & Geneva: World Council of Churches, 1981.

von Balthasar, H. Urs., *Explorations in Theology I: The Word Made Flesh*. San Francisco: Ignatius Press, 1989.
Theo-Drama, Vol. III, San Fransisco: Ignatius Press, 1992.
Explorations in Theology III: Creator Spirit. San Francisco: Ignatius Press, 1993.

Wainright, A.W., *The Trinity in the New Testament*. London: SPCK, 1962.

Ware, K., *The Orthodox Way*. London: Mowbrays, 1979.

Ware, K. & Davey, C. (eds), *Anglican-Orthodox Dialogue: The Moscow Statement Agreed by the Anglican-Orthodox Joint Doctrinal Commission 1976*. London: SPCK, 1977.

Weinandy, T., *Does God Change?: The Word's Becoming in the Incarnation*. Petersham, MA: St. Bede's Publications, 1985.
In the Likeness of Sinful Flesh: An Essay on the Humanity of Christ. Edinburgh: T&T Clark, 1993.
'The Immanent and Economic Trinity', *The Thomist* 57/4 (1993) 655–66.

Widdicombe, P., The Fatherhood of God from Origen to Athanasius. Oxford: Clarendon Press, 1994

Wojtyla, K., *The Acting Person*. London: D. Reidel Publishing Company, 1979.

Wong, J.H.P., 'The Holy Spirit in the Life of Jesus and of the Christian', *Gregorianum* 73 (1992) 57–95.

Yarnold, E., 'The Trinitarian Implications of Luke and Acts', *The Heythrop Journal* VII (1966) 18–32.

Young, F.M., *From Nicaea to Chalcedon: A Guide to the Literature and its Background*. London: SCM, 1983.

Zizioulas, J.D., *Being as Communion*. London: Darton, Longman and Todd, 1985.

INDEX

Made in the USA
Lexington, KY
02 September 2014